Tempus ORAL HISTORY *Series*

Leicester
Voices

The boathouse at Belgrave.

Tempus ORAL HISTORY *Series*

Leicester
Voices

Cynthia Brown

TEMPUS

Horse-drawn tram in use before the introduction of electric trams in 1904.

First published 2002

Tempus Publishing Limited
The Mill, Brimscombe Port,
Stroud, Gloucestershire, GL5 2QG

British Library Cataloguing in Publication Data.
A catalogue record for this book is available from the British Library.

ISBN 0 7524 2657 5

Typesetting and origination by Tempus Publishing Limited
Printed in Great Britain by Midway Colour Print, Wiltshire

Contents

London Road in 1961.

Introduction

This book makes no claim to be a comprehensive history of Leicester over the past 100 years or so. The extracts from recordings have been selected to illustrate different aspects of life in the city, including its own particular experience of two world wars, and to suggest something of how and why it has changed.

At the beginning of the twentieth century, Leicester had a population of just over 200,000. Its main manufacturing industries were hosiery, footwear and engineering, which have all declined significantly in the last decades of the twentieth century under the impact of changes in the national and world economy. The hosiery trade was a large employer of women, many of whom – contrary to the practice in other areas of employment - continued to work after marriage.

In addition to these staple industries was a range of other trades such as printing, chemicals and confectionery, while the extracts in the book also reflect a significant increase in services such as teaching, nursing, transport, office work and retailing.

Alongside those of childhood and schooldays, memories of Leicester's shops feature strongly in the recordings – from the multitude of small corner shops, to specialist food shops such as Simpkin & James, and large department stores such as Lea's, and Lewis's with its landmark tower.

Some of the strongest memories are of poverty and the poor health and housing which so often accompanied it. According to a League of Nations report in 1936, Leicester was the second wealthiest city in the world – an accolade which has itself become part of local folklore. However, oral testimony clearly demonstrates how unevenly this wealth (calculated on average household income) was actually distributed, and how this limited people's access in turn to consumer goods, holidays, and commercial entertainment.

Nevertheless, Leicester's relative prosperity from the later nineteenth century has continued to attract migrants from rural areas, and from other parts of Britain and beyond, in search of employment and 'something better' in the way of social contacts, education and future prospects. As some of the extracts in the final section of the book suggest, Leicester has also become home over the years to many people seeking refuge from religious or political persecution, or the disruptive effects of war.

Oral testimony is one of the most valuable sources of information about the recent past. It may take the form of eye-witness accounts, but can also include folklore, songs and stories passed on by word of mouth – and while it is most commonly used to preserve the knowledge and understanding of older people, there is a lot to be gained from interviewing younger generations as well.

Memory can be unreliable, of course, and the quality of the material will also vary according to the skill of the interviewer. Nevertheless, the recorded memories and opinions of individuals can provide us with new information which is not available through documentary sources. They can offer different perspectives on familiar subjects, and give us invaluable insights into people's feelings and how they interpret their own experiences. Many of the oral history projects set up in the 1980s and 90s were seen as giving a 'voice' to people who have been excluded from more 'conventional' histories, and this is reflected in the earlier recordings in the East Midlands Oral History Archive collections which have a clear bias towards working class oral testimony.

The extracts in this book have been edited only so far as necessary for ease of reading, without in any way changing the sense of what was said. Dates of birth are indicated where contributors have given their permission, but some declined to do so. In a small number of cases, contributors have chosen to remain anonymous, and are identified in this way in the text.

The extracts in this book are just a small sample of the recordings in the East Midlands Oral History Archive, a three year Heritage Lottery funded project to create the first large-scale collection of oral history recordings for Leicestershire and Rutland. The project is supported by the Centre for Urban History at the University of Leicester, the Record Office for Leicestershire, Leicester and Rutland, and the museums and libraries services of Leicester City Council and Leicestershire County Council.

The Archive brings together a number of existing collections, including those of the Leicester Oral History Archive, the Community History archive of Leicester City Libraries, the Mantle collection from North West Leicestershire, and the sound archive of BBC Radio Leicester, as well as smaller collections deposited by individuals and local organizations.

New recordings made since the start of the project in March 2001 are also being added to the archive, which is expected to number around 4,000 items by the end of March 2004. All the recordings will be deposited in the Record Office for Leicestershire, Leicester and Rutland, and are currently being catalogued and copied, both to improve public access to them, and to conserve them for future reference. The East Midlands Oral History Archive catalogue is online at http://www.le.ac.uk/emoha/catalogue.html.

In addition to all the contributors themselves, I would like to thank Angela Cutting and Joyce Mills at the Community History section of Leicester City Libraries for permission to quote from recordings, and for providing many of the photographs included in the book. Particular thanks are also due to my colleagues at the East Midlands Oral History Archive, Sarah Ferrier, Lesley Gill, Tristram Hooley, Colin Hyde, Mandy Morris and Chrissy Thornhill, and one of our volunteers, Faye Minter, for all their help in identifying suitable recordings, scanning images, and reading and commenting on the text. We hope that the end product will evoke still more memories on the part of those who read the book.

Cynthia Brown
Project Manager
East Midlands Oral History Archive

1 Growing Up

Christmas party at the Cascelloid Company of Leicester.

Christmas stockings

At Christmas time, we hung our stocking of course, and we got a sixpenny stocking, network stocking, we got a rosy-cheeked apple, we got an orange which had only just come into season, and we got from my father a bright new penny from the bank. Probably a sixpenny box of bricks, coloured bricks. My four sisters, they received a sixpenny flaxen-haired doll from Germany. That's what we got on Christmas Day.

Mr S. Coleman

Kings of the street!

I remember one Christmas I had a doll's house, but that was only because my

A visit from Santa.

Displays in the windows

Christmas was always a good time. All the shops had figures in them – displays in the windows with figures moving. We used to think it was marvellous. Lewis's, the Co-op, they used to have the grotto. As a boy I had sweets and that sort of thing as presents, train sets with Hornby trains. And if you'd still got it the next year you'd get a few new coaches or carriages to add to it, or some extra rails.

Dennis Britten

Sugar pigs and pianos

Nowadays you'd have a fit and say 'think of the children's teeth'. But we didn't have many sweets in those days, but a sugar pig every Christmas was good! They were pink or white with a little tail, a string tail, I think it was. More often than not there'd be somebody on the piano or we'd have guessing games and that sort of thing, all those old games, if there were enough of you gathered round to play them. Snakes and Ladders, those kinds of games, but not the elaborate ones that you see now, no way, just ordinary cardboard in a cardboard box. Lotto, and that sort of game, fairly simple. We didn't have a lot, as you would say presents, compared with nowadays. But we had a lovely day. We went to one grandparents' for Christmas dinner, and the other set of grandparents for Christmas tea. And we finished up (everyone had a piano then, you know) with a nice musical evening. Crackers and things like that. Oh yes, we had some happy Christmases.

Blanche Harrison

grandfather was a carpenter, coach-builder. He worked down at the Transport in the carpentry, and my Dad was a painter and decorator. My Grandpa made the house, and my Dad decorated it, put paper on like bricks and painted it, you know. I remember that vividly. I once had a doll's cot. My Grandpa made that as well. People used to try to make what they could because they simply hadn't got the money to buy what a child wanted, and you just hoped and prayed you got what you wanted, and if you were very lucky, you did. The thing was, everyone was the same. I did have a doll's pram, but it wasn't a new one, it was second hand. My Grandpa made my brother and I a scooter, a wooden scooter with wooden wheels. And we were kings of the street!

Blanche Harrison

Twopence halfpenny a week

I got twopence a week from my dad and a halfpenny from my grandma, my mum's mum, and believe you me it went quite a long way in those days. Sweets, probably, perhaps an ice cream, I can't think now what I did spend it on, and we thought we were well off. We really thought we were as well off as any of them, any of the other children.

Blanche Harrison

No pocket money

We didn't get pocket money. You were given money to go and get something. If you were going to the pictures you got threepence, if you were going to the sweet shop you got a penny. You didn't have money as such, because there was a lot of unemployment in the 1930s. It was a bit rough for some people.

Dennis Britten

'Cop shop'

We had comics, Chips, I think. Weary Willy and Tired Tim, they were a couple of tramps, and I remember that whenever they were taken off to the Police Station there'd be a finger post pointing 'Cop Shop'. It stuck with me. I always call the Police Station a 'Cop Shop'. Of course, the other kids would have a Dandy and a Beano, the Champion and Rover. Rover was great because there was always a story in it about the war. The one I remember was 'The Exploits of Rockfist Rogan of the RAF', and of course there was some real bloodthirsty exploits every week. You couldn't wait for it to come out! It was great.

John Howlett

American comics

We used to collect comics, one would have a different comic and we'd swap them.

A favourite toy.

Sharing comics.

That was a regular thing. During the war especially we used to love it if we could manage to get these American comics, with Flash Gordon and Mandrake the Magician in, but they were very hard to come by, I could never afford to have them bought me. I mean, I don't know where people got them from, but you did eventually get hold of the odd one, so I used to enjoy them.

Iris Smith

When dad came home

The only money I can remember getting was half a crown when my Dad came home. We used to get half a crown, my sister and me, which is a lot of money. You saved some at the bank at school, 2d or 3d, and the rest you'd spend on sweets. They didn't come off rations till about 1953. You'd get a comic somehow, you'd perhaps buy a couple, then you'd swap. Some comics were worth more than others, you know, like the Beano. You got two of the others for one of them.

Anonymous male contributor (1)

We didn't know we were poor

Families at that time, who lived in the same area, all kind of helped each other. Mother worked for a cigar manufacturer, and when Mum wasn't there we went to Grandma's. She was always there across the street. We had no cars, you know. You would say it was poor nowadays, but we didn't know we were poor as children. I didn't realise we were poor. There were just four of us, and there were many families with many more children.

Blanche Harrison

The orphanage

The orphanage was on the Fosse Road, Fosse Road Central, and it was there for many, many years. While I was at school, every Easter my mother used to send word to my teacher to find out how many pupils there were, how many orphans I should say, at the orphanage, and she used to send every child a new-laid brown egg for Easter Sunday morning. And after Easter, every child used to put their signatures on the end of this letter thanking my mother for the kindness in sending these eggs. So each one had a nice fresh egg for Easter Sunday morning.

Every little orphan had the same type of apron, it was just a plain apron that covered the whole of the dress. Boys and girls all wore the same apron so that there was no difference in how they felt, each child was treated exactly the same. They used to teach them there, there were little desks and everything. They were all there, so they must have had the teachers there too, to teach them. We used to give concerts there every year, which was a great delight to the orphans, because they did look really poor. I mean, they'd got a home, and had got shelter, but it was very, very sparse in those days.

Mrs C. Tebbutt

No socks

I remember big families were the order of the day. Five or six kids was quite common. Lots of kids didn't have any shoes or socks or anything, and in later years I met one fellow from one of these big families, and he said there were never enough socks to go round, so all the kids that went to work had first choice as to what socks were available, and the kids that went to school had the rest, but there was never enough.

Mr R. Issitt

Local children in the 1920s.

Ragged children

There was two houses each side of the entry, and course my Mum had to do work, she went out scrubbing to get money for buying dinners, you know, and this neighbour used to look after me till I went to school, or in the holidays. They were very good. I mean, although we were poor I had a happy childhood. We always had enough to eat, things like that, but I had hand-me-downs where I had to wear other children's clothes, but I was grateful for it. That was a way of life.

When I went to school, children were ragged, and they were sort of penalised, everybody seemed to take it out on them, and some of the teachers too, but thinking about it now, it wasn't the children's fault. I mean, it was awful for them, but I can remember seeing boys with their trousers all bare bottom, little boots that were all worn down, elbows out of their jumpers, and in school, of course, you've sort of got 'they're dirty, you don't want much to do with them', but really that was awful because it wasn't their fault. As you got older, you realised how awful that was for

13

Dolls made by the Cascelloid Company of Leicester.

those children, and they couldn't help it that they were dressed like that. And it's where the fathers had a belt, you could see the fathers wearing the belt, and they'd be hit by them, sometimes they would, you know. It was a hard life, but they didn't know anything different.

Iris Smith

The pawnshop

In Conduit Street, next door to the school, was a very large pawnshop, and mothers used to wash their children's clothing, iron them, and take them into the pawnshop on Monday morning to get a few shillings, and retrieve them again on Saturday.

Mr S. Coleman

I loved my childhood

My friend Joyce, her mum worked, unlike most of our mums, who didn't because our dads worked, but mine didn't have much money. So Joyce was rich. She used to bring sugar mice to school and we used to have feasts on the back row, on the desks in our class. That was wonderful, that was. But although we hadn't got very much money, and although we were most of us extremely poor, it was brilliant. I loved my childhood, but I was fed up because we hadn't any money and I couldn't go on any Sunday school outings or things like that.

Jackie Harvey

A smashing table

We were always very fortunate, very fortunate. We used to have a smashing table, always plenty of lovely meat. And then we used to have a lovely big ham, and a side of bacon hanging in the living room, so we used to carve it off when we wanted it. And Mum always used to make loads and loads of wine. Beetroot wine, parsnip wine, hedgeshoot wine, any wine, anything you mention and my Mum used to make the wine.

Mrs C. Tebbutt

Getting your head down

I went to school when I was five. I went to Mantle Road School. I can remember the place in the school where I sat. We all had to have a sleeping quarter-of-an-hour. We sat at an ordinary desk with like a table at the back

Children at the Day Nursery on Saffron Lane Estate in the 1950s.

of us, and this table came over us and clipped onto the desk. And the teacher used to say to us, 'put your arms across like that and put your head down', and we all had to have a quarter-of-an-hour's rest. I remember the maypole which boys and girls used to dance round. We did what we used to call the plait, and this plait was done to music, you see, with teacher playing piano.

Cecil Harris

She told me all the answers!

I went to St Saviour's School, a church school. As an infant we sat on the floor - no desks in those days. The school was financed by the church, and we paid a penny a week towards the upkeep of the school. I enjoyed school. It was a mixed school, and my cousin sat at the side of me. She was clever and I wasn't, so she told me all the answers! I wasn't clever, but I was brilliant at maths, and that stood me all through my life. At nine o'clock in the morning we assembled in the school yard, a whistle blew at five minutes to nine, and at nine o'clock we marched upstairs, and the first half-hour of the day we had prayers, the Lord's Prayer and a lecture and a hymn, then we dispersed to our classes. The headmaster sat at the desk in the centre of the big room, watching everybody.

In those days there was reading, writing and arithmetic. That was it, really. In the

15

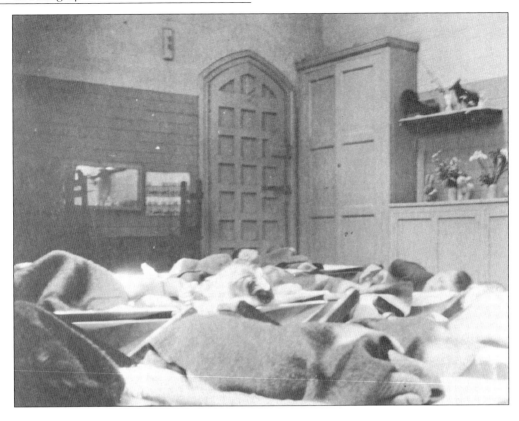

Afternoon nap at St Matthew's Infants School in the 1940s.

Infants we had slates and a slate pencil. Then when we got to the Seniors, we had one exercise book that had to last us twelve months. The girls didn't have the cane. They were stood in the corner for five minutes if they were naughty. You see, the parents of the kiddies were big church people, and it was more or less a family affair.

Herbert Weston

Chewing gum

I can remember starting school, I think I was about three and a half, at Ellis Avenue in the Tinies. I remember one day I had been naughty with a friend sitting near me. A lot of girls had long hair then, and we were sitting in front of each other, and my friend and I, I think it was chewing gum or something, stuck it on this girl's hair, so we were made to sit in the hall in full view of everyone and get this stuff off the girl's hair. I mean, the poor girl had to suffer as well as us. You were put outside the classroom when you were naughty, stand there where they could all see you.

Blanche Harrison

No helpers

I came to teach in St Matthew's Infants School in September 1939. All the schools were closed in the whole area until they'd got shelters, so we just had to walk round the district two by two, so I got to know the whole district in about three weeks. So we walked round, and told the children to go home and fetch their gas masks, as they had to have their coats and gas masks with them all the time. After three weeks they'd managed to open schools part-time. What they did to us was to open the cellars of the old Taylor Street School, which had been built as a factory but never finished, and so it had the semi-basement as factories do.

I had thirty children and no helpers. You managed them, it was hard work, but you managed them. You had to put them to bed in the afternoon in little folding beds, and you had to change the sheets on a Friday, every sheet had to be changed! I think you'd turn them round one week and take them all off the next week, and put on fresh ones and send them home to be washed. All the children wore nursery overalls which all had to go home every week to be washed, and you did your own secretarial work because there weren't any secretaries.

Margaret Zientek

Home in a funeral cab

One November evening at half four we came out of school and it was getting dark, and I was playing around in the cloakroom, with a friend I suppose. I was late getting home, and I remember running down Melton Road, and they were cobbles, the streets, and I ran across Halkin Street, and slipped, and there was a baker's cart. It's a

One way of getting around!

good job he was empty because had he been full I would have broken some bones. He was coming round the corner and I was nipping across thinking 'Oh I'm late, I'll be in trouble' and I slipped and the wheel went over my back and my shoulder. And of course he stopped and he saw that I was alright. There was a funeral cab going down the Melton Road and it stopped for some reason, so I was taken home in a funeral cab. It was dusk by that time, and he'd got his lamps on, and my mother was expecting my young sister at that time, the one who was born on Christmas Day, and it was my fault because Mother saw this funeral cab outside the house, she came to the front door, and there was this funeral cab. She had such a shock, she couldn't think what had happened. But I was alright, except for my coat which was messed up, so I was told off for that. Once they knew I was alright, I was in trouble for messing about at school!

Blanche Harrison

Quite an adventure

It was quite an adventure to go on your bicycle down there, what is now Glenfield Road, because you had to open all these gates. The first one was what we called the Cornfield. That had got a black path, and I fell off my bike looking at a pheasant, I've still got the black path in my knee! When we used to go to school, though, we had to walk, and the golf links were there too, and they used to have sheep on them in the winter. You'd run into the sheep in the dark, and also when we went to school we fell down the bunkers where the snow had all gone, 'cos we don't get snow like that nowadays, and you'd end up right over your wellies in this bunker.

Marjorie Smart

Girls' high school

It was super really. My sister Phyllis and myself, we went to the Hinckley Road High

Bendbow Rise Infants' School, 1945.

School, a girls' high school that was run by Mrs Ada Ward, that was on the Hinckley Road. We never had half a day when the Council schools had their half day because our headmistress, she always thought no, you couldn't have half a day with the other children. It was very, very nice, it was opposite Dulverton Road, I think the majority of that property now is flats, but in those days, I mean, it was, oh, well respected and a very nice area all that end. We used to always go so that we'd be in school when the bell from the Wyggeston Hospital started to ring. That was at five and twenty past nine in the morning. And then we had from twelve till two for lunch, and then we finished at four o'clock in the afternoon. And it really was very, very nice, very nice indeed.

There would be about thirty pupils altogether, and occasionally through the summer months Miss Ward would hire a horse and brake with two horses, and take us all to Bradgate for the day. Some would go upstairs into the open part of the brake, and others would be inside. And of course that was a great treat for all of us to go on this horse and brake. It was lovely. We all wore uniform - during the summer months it was a panama, with the band round the hat and the GHS, Girls' High School, on the front, and your blazers with the same monogram on the pocket. We were all in uniform.

Mrs C. Tebbutt

Bullies

I completed Standard 6 at twelve and a half years, did exams and qualified to attend by an examination what was then known as a secondary school. Alderman Newton's and Wyggeston, etc. My parents couldn't afford to let me go as I would not have left and got a job at fourteen. Whilst the Head at Old Milton Street, Mr Boulter, was quite a gentleman but rather stern - he gave us strokes of the cane and our name entered in the red book - some of the teachers were bullies. I remember particularly one who we pelted with pieces of wood which we brought from our woodworking class in Orchard Street.

Albert Hall

Very progressive

I found the headmaster at Gateway was very progressive. It was really a good school because over a four or five year period we could try many different trades out, because we were sited very near to the School of Art and Technology. And we used to have classes in the Art & Tech on all the aspects of industry. We'd do an engineering course, and a course on knitwear where we made each other a pair of socks, and boot and shoe, slippers and that kind of thing. There was even a kind of commercial art department. So it was a good grounding for bringing people into industry, like a pre-course for an apprenticeship, because apprenticeships were still around in those days.

Colin Green

University College

I was there from 1924-26. I wanted to teach. At that time there were very few students here really, but my father was determined not to send me away. We had a very good time. Everything was beginning. It really was like building a new building, you know what I mean, building it up. Everything that happened was new. We tried to start a badminton club, and the only place we could find, the ceiling was too low, so we couldn't run badminton there. We tried to have a hockey match and they ran out of people, and they said 'can't you play hockey?', and I said 'never touched a hockey stick in my life, I couldn't possibly'. 'It's quite alright, my dear', they said, 'you just hit it hard through the goal! Hold the right hand of the stick up, you know, do all that and then push it through'. I did all that and got a goal!

They'd only got nine students when they began, and they were very enterprising because they were older than usual, because they'd been put off going to college because of the war and their parents' worry. Of the nine students, one was a man, a poor lone man. It lasted for a year, just one poor lone man and eight other students. They got a drama society going almost at once, and it was while I was still there, they had people like C.P. Snow. He was very much the 'father' of the little group we were in. He started a chess club, and he started a magazine. He was also a very fine cricketer. He of course went on to great things.

There weren't any Halls of Residence as such a lot of the people were local, you see, but some of them came through by train from Northampton or various places round about. One of the youngsters said when we were there, 'yes, there weren't many of us, but we were young, and it was fun, and we felt to be pioneers'. You could get a very small sum towards your education. The fees were £20 a year to cover the whole thing. It was almost like being in a small private school. You got a lot of attention.

They had a huge bazaar in De Montfort Hall, to provide money. My sister was to be a French fisherman. This was when she was still at school, and one of the staff came along who'd been to Brittany, and she'd got a man there, a fisherman, to give her the right garb to wear. Mother's face when she thought she was to wear this thing, it had never been washed or anything! She just had to get to work and boil it up.

Nora Waddington

The original University College Leicester, formerly a lunatic asylum.

2 Play and Pastimes

A family picnic at Swithland Woods in 1920.

No playing out on Sundays

We weren't allowed to play out on Sundays, no way, because, although I was Christened in the Church of England at St Mark's, we used to go to the Methodist Chapel, Belgrave Hall it was called. And the Methodists always had an anniversary every year, and my auntie made my dress. All the girls had a new dress, and the boys had a sailor suit or whatever, and that was the big day of the year because we had a new dress, and all the parents used to come, and for once the place was packed. Always it was in May. We looked forward to that. It was always a pretty dress.

Blanche Harrison

Bank Holiday Monday

The Bank Holiday Monday was a ritual whereby all of the local children or youths and girls, and families for that matter, would walk from where we lived in New Road to Bradgate Park. Every Bank Holiday Monday. Not only would we walk there, we would walk back, and in between times run around the park, so you can imagine that we'd be very, very tired when we got back. But we'd take a jam sandwich, and probably a lemonade bottle filled with cold tea wrapped up in a sock. That would be a wonderful day out as far as we were concerned. In the season we'd walk out to Swithland Woods and collect bluebells and bring them back. Of course they never lasted long. Next day when you looked at them they were all dead.

Mr G. Stacey

A circular walk

Going up Imperial Avenue, we could go down to the bottom of the rough track, after the Fosse Road corner, down to a footpath which actually is now Braunstone Avenue. As boys we used to walk along that path, as an outing. We'd go right into Braunstone through the fields. Go by Braunstone Hall, Braunstone Lake, and turn right, and just inside on the right-hand side was another little lane which led to perhaps one or two houses, and to a blacksmith's shop. This

Crook's carrier service from Leicester to Loughborough and Shepshed.

blacksmith's shop was working, by the way. We then walked onto another footpath which lay diagonally across the fields towards Hinckley Road, and that made a nice circular walk for us.

William Lenton

Trips to the country

On some occasions, we'd got a trap, we used to go over to my aunt's at Desford, and then we'd come back, oh probably half eleven at night, and Dad would stable the horses, and other times we would go on the carrier's cart to my aunt at Peckleton, which would call at Mrs Green's, the greengrocer in Dunster Street, and they would pick us up, and we used to go all the way over, I would imagine it would be for about twopence those days, that they would charge, because they were taking all the green stuff and bringing greengrocery to Mrs Green.

Mrs C. Tebbutt

Playing dangerously

We used to go up the chapel roof. It had a big steep roof, and we used to go up there for a shilling on bare feet. I never did it myself, but one or two did for a shilling, which was a lot of money. Of course, there wasn't so many trains, it would be hours between trains, and we used to put nails on the line to flatten them to make arrow heads. If you stood at the top, it was a steep drop. I remember someone, he was coming up the bank and stumbled and there was a train coming, and he rolled all the way to the bottom and we thought that was the end of him, but he got to the gully, thank God, else he would have been dead.

Anonymous male contributor (1)

Out for hours

We were out for hours. We'd sit in Tick Tock Park where there was a couple of parkies who'd be brewing their tea up, and we'd sit in there until it was well dark and we'd go. And I can remember taking my brother. He was born in 1946, so he'd only be a baby in about 1948, and walking all the way through to Meadow Gardens because we'd got friends on Meadow Gardens. Well actually we'd got some boyfriends on Meadow Gardens if the truth be known, and we were there for hours, and then I'd wheel him back again and it would be getting dark.

Our parents never bothered where we were. They never worried because it was safe. There was no worry at all. Whole gangs of us would go up to 'Sandhills' where the Eyres Monsell is now. That was all fields, and there was nothing there at all. And we used to play up there, whole gangs of us, and we would play in the water. No one was ever drowned or anything. The parents were quite happy. I mean, you just said where you were going and that would be it. So, I mean, it has changed.

Jackie Harvey

Guttering

We used to play guttering in the street. We used to stand at this drain with a bat, and we had sides – it doesn't matter how many, six, say – and the six used to field up there. Well, the first one used to throw the ball at you, and we used to hit it as hard as we could, and whoever was fielding used to take it to the gutter and try to get it as near as they could to the drain by rolling it along the gutter. If whoever threw it got dead on the guttering, you were out, but if it stuck there you used to say six and then they used to put their feet one in front of the other from the ball to the grating, and if you got it in your six you won,

Elston Fields on Saffron Lane Estate, commonly known as 'Tick Tock' Park.

you counted them as runs, but if you didn't, you were out. We could play for hours till we got fetched to go to bed. It would be about nine or ten o'clock.

Anonymous male contributor (1)

Gone like rabbits

The gangs used to meet on the corner of the street to play cards. They would spread out a couple of jackets, the cards would come out, and the gangs would sit round the cards. Two lookouts looked for the policemen, and if, as and when, they were spotted, you would never see these people. They were gone like rabbits in the little hovels, down entries, over garden walls, all sorts of things.

Mr G Stacey

Horses and carts

You could step off the pavement. You needn't even look right and left. This business of looking right or left came in later years. There were very, very few motor cars, mostly horses and carts. For instance, the Midland Railway, all their deliveries were by a van and a big dray horse. You'd stand about, meet your friends, have a chat with them. The pavements were pretty clear. It was like a country town would be now, if as busy.

Mona Lewis

No cars to knock you over

If you saw one car in the street, that's all you saw. We actually played in the streets - Tin Lurkey, Cops and Robbers and that sort of thing. You could throw a stick and play a football game. There were no cars to come into you and knock you over or for you to get into trouble with. There were big streets and there were so few cars. I can remember in the 1950s we always used to seem to have extra long skipping ropes - they went right across the street, I presume it was someone's washing line or something like that.

Jackie Harvey

Playing ball and skipping

In those days it was double ball, and you progressed to triple ball, spending hours and hours and hours playing ball up against the shop wall on the corner of the street. Hours! You'd throw the ball up against the wall, and you'd clap in between each, and see how many claps you could do, and there were various games and also over arm and under arm. Yes, there were all sorts of rhymes and competitions as to how long you could keep it going - and then see if you could bring the

Children playing in St Peter's Road in the early twentieth century.

third ball in as well! There were big skipping games, because of course in those days, we're talking here about the late '50s, you could play in the street, out in the road, and you used to literally have huge great skipping lines, clothes lines, going across the street, and you'd just keep turning and turning and scoot off every now and then to let a car by.

Lesley Gill

Poddy one two three

Poddy one two three. Have you heard of that one? It's like a hide and seek game with a poddy post, where the person who's doing the catching has to stay, and the other people run away and hide, and while the

catcher's away looking for everyone you have to go to the poddy post and say 'poddy one two three', and if you're back safe, you are the first one back – was it the first one back? I can't remember now – was the winner or whatever.

Clare Speller

You can't play with us

I got to Leicester and I was very unhappy because I'd always played with boys, but when we got to Leicester it was segregated, and boys played with boys and girls played with girls. And I couldn't understand this, I can remember that very clearly, just not understanding. I'd run out in the street and want to play with them and they'd say 'go away, you're just a little girl, you can't play with us', and I'd have to go off and then learn how to play girls' games.

Lesley Gill

British bulldog

British bulldog was kind of a violent game, whereby you'd start with one person in the middle of the playground and everyone else lined up at one end of the playground, and that one person would select someone from the line and that person would have to get past them and get to the home base on the other side of the playground. Now, if the

Cricket was generally seen as a boys' game – but sometimes the girls were allowed to play!

person caught them, then they joined them and they became part of the catching team, and then they'd select someone else, to a point when they'd got enough in the middle that they'd say 'OK, everyone', and then they'd just try to grab as many people as possible, you know.

But it was always a bit scary, British Bulldog, really. You kind of liked all the twisting and turning because when you're a kid you like throwing yourself around and showing how fast you are, and exploring your physical abilities, I suppose.

Mark Jones

A clapping game

We play a clapping game and it's about my friends and family. My sister Alice made it up and we added things to it:

Mum is a teacher. Sit down, shut up.
My nephew is a DJ. Scratch, scratch, scratch, scratch.
My niece is a singer. La la, yeah, yeah.
My sister is a dancer. Tap, tap, tap, tap.

I like it because we worked on a bit of it, and then we added loads more, and it's fun to do because we get to sing it and then you do it with your friends, so lots of people can join in.

Year 5 children at Shaftesbury Junior School,
Leicester

Cylinder records

Entertainment was confined really to what you could do locally. We had a very large gramophone, huge horn on the thing with a sound box, and also, they weren't the flat records, they were cylinder records.

Mr G. Stacey

St Matthew's Infants' School playground in the 1940s.

Concert parties and playhouses

There was a few concert parties in the town, and Caitlin's Pierrots used to come and do a turn at the old Temperance Hall, long since pulled down, opposite Northampton Street. And they did a season there. Will Caitlin was a Leicester man, and they were excellent entertainers. There were five playhouses in Leicester, the Palace, the Opera House, the Theatre Royal, the Pavilion, and the Empire. The Empire was a tiny little music hall. You could stand on the stage and almost touch the gallery, it was so small. It later became the Hippodrome. The Opera House in Silver Street was a very good place, and I always remember going in later years to see musical comedy. We used to queue in a yard or shed, and then you went up stone stairs one by one, till gradually you went to heights of the 'gods', which was ninepence, in the gallery. There you would sit on a bare board, no seats. If it was a popular show there would be people waiting outside, and a man used to come along and say 'move up please, move up', so you were gradually pushed into a little small space. It was uncomfortable, very hot, no cloakroom to put your coats, but once the lights went up, the orchestra tuned in and the curtains parted, then you were led into another world. It was rather marvellous.

Mr W. E. Burton

27

Travelling cinema

The travelling cinema was drawn along the roads by a traction engine, and went for miles and miles and miles. It would be a day's job to get to where they were going from early morning, a good long day.

Mr A. Holland

Silent films

My first job was at the Floral Hall in Belgrave Gate, next door to the Leicester Palace, in late 1928. Of course in those days it was all silent pictures, and at the time electric motors had only just come in to run the projectors. Very often, when the motors had failed, I used to have to turn the handle to run the projector from two o'clock until ten o'clock in the evening. We used to have a pianist there, playing for the silent pictures. When you got the cowboys he used to play the fast music to match the cowboys, which proved very entertaining. In them days, of course, they were mostly cowboy pictures. Fred Thompson, the cowboy, and Silver King, his horse. Also Tom Mix and Charlie Chaplin, which people loved.

Mr. A. Warren

Twopenny rushes

I used to go to the matinee on Saturday afternoons at the Hippodrome. It cost twopence. Upstairs was threepence, and if you were sat downstairs they'd throw things down on top of you, so I asked my mother if I could have the threepence to go upstairs, you know. We used to go and see the serials, oh yes, that was a great afternoon out. I remember going with my friends, we decided to go round all the cinemas, just to visit and then say we'd been in them. The Star had got

a bad name on Belgrave Gate - that was somewhere down near St Mark's Church - and we'd heard they called it a flea pit, so we went to the Star this time,. and we went to the box office and said 'how much is it upstairs?', and she said 'there isn't an upstairs!'. But it was fun trying, just to go round saying we'd been in all of them.

Iris Smith

The Aylestone

There was no balcony at the Aylestone, they used the hill because of the slope. Another favourite pastime at the pictures was to get a laggy band on your fingers with a bit of paper and stick it through the beam. You'd get chucked out for that. Another thing we used to do at the pictures was enter the doors on the street, then we went along a long passage to get to the lower prices, then turned left into some doors. Well, we got to these doors and pulled them sharply. The doors at the top used to fly open, and a bloke used to chase us down the street. After about half an hour we'd creep back up and do it again!

Anonymous male contributor (1)

Pubs all the way down

There was the Prince of Wales in Crafton Street, and there was a pub opposite the corner of Wheat Street called the Boot and Shoe Club. Oh, and the Baker's Arms was also in Crafton Street. There were pubs all the way down Wharf Street.

Iris Smith

No music in the pubs

We didn't have music in pubs in Leicester. It was so rowdy, music was condemned and

One of the many pubs in the Wharf Street area.

no one was permitted to sing in a pub at all - we were about the only place in the British Isles that didn't sing! You could go to Nottingham and have a rare old time. It was condemned by the City fathers, and you couldn't even have a solo. You couldn't have a piano. Now you could go to Rothley and have a real old ding-dong there. This was right from the First World War.

Mr S. Coleman

Circus animals

When the circus was being shown at the Palace Theatre, some of the animals were kept in the back area of the Fish and Quart in Church Gate. There would be lions, tigers, horses, ponies, and also seal lions, and invariably as lads we got in the back way and used to go and torment the animals, which wasn't a very kind thing to do.

Mr G. Stacey

Last Fair in Humberstone Gate in 1904.

Humberstone Gate fair

The fair went from Wharf Street nearly up to the Clock Tower, and there were all kinds of sideshows and stalls. We had two fairs, held in May and October. Beyond the fair, roughly where Burton's was, there used to stand two men. One used to sell buns, little buns, three for a penny. He used to say 'come along, my dear, three for a penny, the buns'. The other man had a very elaborate brass-fitted apparatus, almost like a fire engine, and used to sell baked potatoes. You used to pay a penny and he'd give you a hot potato, and in the cold weather you used to buy it to keep your hands warm. He used to sell roast potatoes and black puddings. He did very well too.

Mr E. Andrews

Last fair

My father took me to the fair in Humberstone Gate in 1904, the year the horse tram finished. After that the fair went to Ross Walk for many years. Then it went to Ulverscroft Road.

Mr S. Coleman

Ross Walk

I remember the big fair they used to have down Ross's Walk. Now Ross's Walk is off Belgrave Road. It was a big expanse of waste land, and we used to have what was called the autumn fair, and oh, it was massive. There were roundabouts, coconut shies,

Brandy Snap stall at Ross Walk Fair.

Safe bathing – the paddling pool at Abbey Park.

Western Park, Leicester.

everything, it was a massive thing. It went from Leicester to Nottingham. We used to have a fair in Nicholas Street. This fair was almost next door to the Foresters' Institute, and we spent quite a lot of time there.

Cecil Harris

Jumping in the river

People jumping in the river at Abbey Park and swimming, it still goes on now when you get scorching hot weather. That was one of my main problems, especially at weekends when I used to position myself at the bridge and sit there for probably two hours because it was a central point and people knew where to contact me, and the kids used to just jump off the bridge into the river – the deepest part. I got a lot of abuse and the council put signs up to say that this water was unfit for bathing, no swimming allowed. But they still do it, it's always been known, swimming in the river further up. It's shallow now, and this is the only place where they do it. Years ago, from the 1900s to 1980, there used to be a main pool there. They had regattas and everything, but it's all changed.

Dave Pick

Western Park

To get to Western Park we got a halfpenny return on the tram. When we used to go to the park, you see, we loved it because of all the gullies up there, but we didn't know what to do with the tickets, so we'd put them in our shoes. Well, you can imagine, after we'd spent a few hours running and racing about, they were nearly disintegrated.

Iris Smith

Abbey Park Show

One of our regular duties was doing the Abbey Park Show. We used to have to work all night on tent patrol because a lot of vandalism was done to the tents. They'd start preparing at least three weeks before the show, erecting tents. Of course the kids used to like to go up and slide on the tents and rip the canvas, so we used to get a bit of overtime. The main attraction at the park then was the gymkhana, the horse show. We used to get the big names, David Broome was here, it was a show on its own, the gymkhana. We also had the dog show in the park as well as the horticultural show. We had the Army, the Air Force and the Navy, but over the years the dog show went to Braunstone Park, and the Army and the Navy stopped coming for political reasons. Towards the end there was less

Fun at the Abbey Park Show.

The Turkey Café, another of Leicester's favourite refreshment places.

than a third of the attractions that had actually started. You used to get in for less than one pound and you could see all these attractions. I really looked forward to the show in those days - I looked forward to working on them because with the wine tent and the Campaign for Real Ale tent, well you can imagine. There used to be a big marquee and flower tents, and it wasn't just Leicester City Council that used to exhibit, it was Birmingham and all the others.

Dave Pick

Afternoon tea

There were endless cafes where you could go in and have a coffee or tea. It was a thing to go out and have afternoon tea, and you'd have a nice pot of tea, a little carton of cream, a dish of cakes – and I mean a real dish of cakes, it was piled high, you didn't just have one brought round to you. Scones and butter and perhaps cream and strawberries. You met your friends in town, but of course nowadays I suppose that has gone, and the cafes have closed, because the majority of women go to work.

Mona Lewis

Coffee Houses

In 1900 there was the Leicester Coffee House Company. Beautiful buildings - one in Granby Street, one in Campbell Street, one at the corner of Wharf Street, one in Cobden Street, one in Church Gate and one in Highcross Street. Coffee was a penny, tea a penny, cocoa a penny, and a big wad of cake, not quite a cob, more like a bun, that was a penny. Marble-topped tables, and sawdust on the floor.

Mr S. Coleman

Kardomah Café

Inside Adderley's was the Kardomah Café, and we used to go down there to smell the coffee. They used to roast coffee down in the basement – ground it and roast it down there.

Frank Smith

Socials at the Secular Society

We had monthly socials – which was a sort of concert – and dancing. You could play Housey Housey, as it was then known, on Sunday before the lectures. We had table tennis, billiards, snooker. We had a cycling club and keep-fit. We used to do little operettas and had a good drama group, outings, discussion classes. We were open 364 days a year, early morning till late at night. You could go any time and get refreshment. The only day we closed was Christmas Day.

Louie Croxtall

Holidays at Hungerton

I was fortunate that some friends of the family were farmers at Hungerton, the Baggrave estate. I used to go there for my holidays. She used to come in every Saturday and bring chickens and eggs and that sort of thing. I used to go there (except if we went to Skegness which was about the farthest we went) from Belgrave Road station.

Dennis Britten

'Foreign' travel

We had to be careful what sort of tickets we issued, because if a person came in for a ticket to Newcastle, for example, we'd have to ask them what train they were going on because certain trains went via Doncaster, and certain trains went by Frickley. With the trains being privately owned, if you issued a ticket via Doncaster, that meant that the London & North-Eastern Railway would get the whole amount of that money, but if you issued a ticket via Frickley, the LMS would claim money for the part of the journey that ran over their line. So we used to say that if we issued a ticket via Doncaster, that was a 'local' ticket. If we issued it via Frickley, it was a 'foreign' ticket. If you ran over another company's line, it was considered a 'foreign' railway ticket.

Albert Lynn

I thought I was sinking!

I was a Tawny Owl in the Brownies, and I was a leader in the Guides. But I gave it up when I was about fifteen because I used to have to go on the parade down the road on Sunday mornings, and used to see all the lads that I knew and they all used to shout to me so I packed it in! We had camp fires and knotting, Morse code and all that sort of thing. I didn't go on holiday till I was nearly twelve years of age. Yarmouth, yes, it was a nice place then, and when I stepped on the sands I thought I was sinking! But I didn't – it was lovely then! There wasn't all those stalls on the front and that sort of thing, just the oyster stalls. I went with my aunt and uncle, and then my cousin.

Anonymous female contributor (1)

Industrial Espionage

Air travel, of course, never entered into the scene. It was rail and sea. Then we realised that coach travel was gradually creeping in. The place these long distance coaches started from was the public house yard, I think it was the Hat & Beaver in Highcross Street. Every morning coaches would leave there for Cheltenham, which connected with other places all over the country. As a lad I was given the job every morning as a sort of industrial spy – I'd have to go out, sort of in disguise, and hang around Highcross Street to find out how many passengers travelled each day on the coach. Then I would have to report back to the manager, and he would send a report to his head office.

Albert Lynn

A visit to Australia

Australia was a lovely place, we went on a visit in 1914. I had an aunt and uncle who lived at a place called Emu Park - there were only 200 inhabitants there. It was on the edge of the bush, and they lived in a great big wooden hut with a little confectionery and sweet shop at the side. They had wire strung across and curtains to make it private at night, but your beds and everything - all in this one hut - were all open. You cooked on a primus stove. At the back of this hut was a high hill and while we were there, there was a drought. There was one water tank, no water laid on, and it came to the stage when we had one bowl of water, and we all washed in that bowl of water, one after the other, and after that we used to save the bowl of water to wash our pots, and then we'd pour what was left on the poor dried-up plants outside. Eventually the drought broke and the rains came, and the torrential rains poured down this hill, through our huts. We were walking in mud and water, and that was just as strange. You either get a drought that dries everything or up, or you're drowned with the heavy rains. But, oh, in ways it was lovely. You could walk over the sands, strip on the sands to your bare skin, go in the sea, and just wallow in the summer.

Mona Lewis

Lectures at the 'Sec'

The lectures at that time were in the big hall upstairs. I was taken when I was eight, staying up late, not to intellectual lectures but to the concerts. We had an orchestra. Bertrand Russell and Annie Besant, I did go and hear Annie Besant. I can see her now stomping up and down the stage with black, woollen stockings. She was small, very small. The Secular Society enriched my life and made me a very tolerant person - because we only had lecturers who were prepared to answer any questions in discussion, which was often the most interesting part of the evening.

Louie Croxtall

Insulting the speakers

We invited a local spiritualist, Miss Eva Lees, whose father was Robert Lees who was supposed to have discovered the identity of Jack the Ripper in the nineteenth century. Well, they were very rude down there at one time. They used to get up and pretty well insult the speakers. We used to have some professors that used to go down, and these people used to be laying the law down, you see, and they didn't like being questioned and criticised. So they said 'I'm not going down there again'. Anyway, Eva Lees had to face this sort of thing, and she was really tough! An old lady with sort of wrinkled stockings like Norah Batty, you know, and she stood up there and she gave as good as they gave her! She really did very well. She put up a good case for spiritualism.

Harold Hammersley

A charabanc outing operated by Griffin's Garage in Gwendolen Road after the First World War – a forerunner of the coach trip.

Old and young on the beach in the 1950s.

3 Working

Shoe room at the Equity footwear co-operative in Western Road, 1929.

Haymaking

My sister and I used to take the horses down to the blacksmith's at the bottom of King Richard's Road, as it was then. We'd wait there until the horses had been shod, and then bring them back to my Dad and he'd take them up to the fields. And when Dad was haymaking, Mother would pack a big basket of goodies, tea and everything, and my sister used to walk up to the fields and take it to Dad while he was mowing and getting the hay all ready. You'd have the hay rakes, about three to four times larger than ordinary garden rakes, and you'd rake all the grass into one complete row right across the fields, and then the next day you would go and turn it over so that the sun dried every bit of it before it was all gathered up. Then it would be put on the float, and we would come back to Sykefield Avenue and we got the huge haystacks there that Dad used to make with my cousin and my uncle.

Mrs C. Tebbutt

Short time

After the First World War my father came back to the firm that he left - boot and shoe manufacturers - but very often he was out of work for weeks, and always on very short time, but he made up any arrears and debts that we had by working full time on piece work in the more prosperous days. My mother had given up her job at Corah at the end of the war because, with five children to look after, she had quite a job on her hands. In fact we did have another baby born, a baby girl, which made our family up to six.

When I left school I was employed at a chemist's called Martin's in Willow Street, who made up fever powders which were well used at that time, and I spent most of my time wrapping up the powder in the little packets which were then sold. I didn't stay there too long, and consequently had jobs in the boot and shoe and the hosiery industry, but with the short time which was operated, and the manner in which we used to be put off as soon as they were on short time, it was necessary to keep finding fresh jobs. I settled down as an apprentice joiner in 1923.

Albert Hall

Labour exchange

In the 1930s there was a sort of long wooden building that used to be something to do with the Labour Exchange, painted green, I think it was. I should think it was almost on the site

Gimson's Correspondence Office at Vulcan Road, around 1930. Office work generally paid less than manufacturing, but carried a higher status.

where the Jewry Wall Museum is. An old-fashioned building with small windows. It was almost on the outskirts in those days.

Marjorie Smart

Taking in washing

At one time my mother took washing in, and I remember once I had to go and take this washing – it was on a Wednesday teatime after school – to a lady on Ross's Walk. Now it was half a crown for two dozen or something like that, and I was told not to leave the house until I had the half crown. When I got round the lady had to wait for her husband to come home and give her the half crown. See, I was told not to come home without it, because that was the middle of the week boost to my mum's money, and it was a lot in those days, you know, half a crown. And then I thought, we must be poor, having to wait for half a crown on a Wednesday.

Blanche Harrison

More money

I worked for Sir Arthur Wheeler when I left school, stockbrokers, doing the circulars and working the addressographs. I got seventeen and six a week. That was good, that's why my mother sent me there – because she wanted the extra money and 'cos father wasn't bringing anything in, and everybody else only got ten shillings a week. But the trouble was at Sir Arthur's you got paid once a month, and every four times a year there's five weeks, but you still only got a month's pay. But you had a couple of tickets that were valued at a pound, I think they were, and you had to save those and draw those out for your holiday. 'Course, I didn't go on holiday, I had to draw them out because Mother needed them, but that's a different story! Then

Mother said I'd got to earn a bit more money, so I went to Woodford's, to treadle the machine and make loose covers for the mattresses, then I learnt how to put the springs in – they used to have a thousand springs in each mattress. We used to put them in with a sort of peg, into slots, long slots they were. The first 'Luxuress' was made for Joseph Johnson. I was bored stiff!

Anonymous female contributor (1)

Learn a trade

I must admit I didn't like school, I mean, they really are the best days of your life, but you don't realise that when you're at school. I couldn't wait to leave to get to work. I went to Ellis Avenue School, and I left there at fourteen. I'd always wanted to serve in a shoe shop, so I got a job in the Co-op in High Street selling shoes, and the starting wage was 18s 6d a week. Well that was quite good, but we had to work till half past six on Friday and Saturday nights. Well, none of my friends worked on Saturdays, not Saturday afternoons, and they didn't want to wait for me when we went out on Saturday evenings, so I sort of got a bit fed up with that, so I left. I worked there for a year, then my mother said to me 'learn a trade', she said, 'even if you don't stay in a factory, learn a trade'. So I learnt to be an overlocker. Then I did pressing, and that's sort of what I did for the rest of my working life.

Iris Smith

Apprenticed at the BU

I got in touch with the BU (British United Shoe Machinery Company) when they were taking on trainees, apprenticeships, so I went along there and they were quite glad for me to sign an apprenticeship, and my

Female hosiery workers at Harrison & Hayes in 1928.

dad was as well, at the time. I got placed with a guy who knew the job inside out, done it all his life, and he took me through the shop, but then came the age of eighteen, and I came out of the apprenticeship to go into the forces, because the way I saw it, if I went in at eighteen I would be out at twenty, whereas I could have been deferred until I was twenty-one. But at twenty-one I would start coming on proper money, because you're only paid a pittance as an apprentice. After I came out of the RAF, the hosiery industry at that time paid very good wages, it was probably the top wage, and it was using machinery again which I'd been used to anyway, you see, so I very quickly picked it up. A knitter in the hosiery and knitwear, I did them both, socks and outerwear and things like that.

Colin Green

Printer's Pie

I started as an apprentice in 1952. Day one you were given a brush and you were told to sweep the floor. That was your first job every morning. Pick all the type up off the floor if there was any there, even between the floorboards 'cos in those days type was made of lead, or lead, antimony and tin, which was precious and valuable so we used to have to pick that up in the morning. Then you used to have what they called a little load of pie, printer's pie, which was a complete mess of different typefaces. You imagine different typefaces with different point sizes, say 6, 8, 10, 12, 14 and so on. Each one of them you'd probably got, even at C. Brooks & Co. that didn't have a big range of typefaces, and you might have four or five different typefaces in one case. So if you finished up with a nice little pile on the floor or on the stone, they'd all got to be sorted and put back into cases.

Keith Dent

Joining the union

I joined the Amalgamated Society of Woodworkers in the last year of my apprenticeship because this was the custom

One of Leicester's foremost engineering companies, Gimson's Main Foundry in Vulcan Road, around 1929.

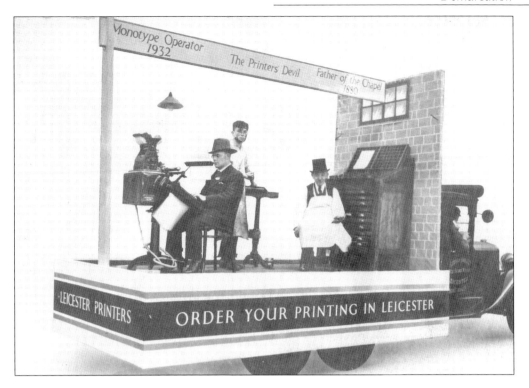

Printing was a major industry in Leicester from the later nineteenth century.

in the firm for which I worked, and I remember my colleagues informing me that as soon as I reached the age of twenty I would have to join. Everybody at the works was in the appropriate union, and this was part of the way of life. I didn't make any objections to it, because although I wasn't an active trade union member, I accepted my responsibility and joined.

Albert Hall

Go and see Jack

I joined the union on my first day at the BU. I was told to 'go and see Jack over there and tell him to give you a form. He's the union bloke'. And I said 'why do I want to be in the union?'. I was told 'you join the union, lad. It'll look

after you'. So I went along and joined the union, the Amalgamated Engineering Union.

Colin Green

Demarcation

It was very union intensified in those days, the printing industry was. The Typographical Association, which I joined when I was sixteen 'cos they had a branch called the Guild of Young Printers. And you joined that and when you finished your apprenticeship at whatever age, twenty-one, you then became a journeyman and you went into the main print union, which was the Typographical Association. You couldn't touch any other job. For example if you were a compositor you did not do any guillotining, you did not do

45

any machine printing, and you did not do any bookbinding. You didn't. Demarcation was that strict.

Keith Dent

Good workers

One of the advantages of being Irish was that you had the reputation of being able to work. Everybody expects you to be a good worker if you're Irish. So generally speaking, in certain lines of work, in transport, in hospital work and anything like that, you were likely to get a job ahead of anybody else, because of the reputation that had been built up by our predecessors. I was a supervisor on the railways for many years, and I was always quite happy to give an Irishman a chance. I was also probably the hardest one on him if he didn't mark up to what he should be. Most of the Irish gangers were rather tough, but expected a lot more from the Irish than they did from other people.

Henry Dunphy

Permission to stay

A girl at my office got married, and she asked the boss's permission to stay in her job. The Managing Director called her to his office where she had a lecture on what her duties were now she was married, but under the circumstances she was allowed to stay. That was more or less the attitude. You married, you stayed at home, you had your children, you looked after your husband and that was the extent of your life. It didn't matter if your husband lost interest in you – you were still his housekeeper. Well, times have changed. A woman can now take her place in life. She can lead a free and responsible life of her own, which is all to the good.

Mona Lewis

Office boy to cashier

I was coming up to the age of fourteen when I left school. I'd got no qualifications, but I left on the Friday and on the Monday I got an interview with a firm in Leicester, a big firm in Leicester, and they gave me some sums to do, which of course were quite easy, and they took me on. Faire Brothers, Rutland Street. John Faire was the senior director – it was a family business – and he took an interest in me, and I was put in the counting house and that's where I stayed. I went from office boy to cashier. I went back to Faire Brothers after the First World War, when I began to climb the ladder there. When I came back from the war, the Secretary said 'well, I can only pay you three pounds'. So that was that. I finished up on £25 a week. I put up thousands of pounds of wages for years, and credit control, and office ledger work and the lot. The wage bill came to £2,000 for the factory, and then there was the warehouse staff. £2,000 a week, I put up.

Herbert Weston

Sheer persistence

My first job was in Kendall's shop – rainwear. In those days you took your umbrella in to be repaired or recovered, you didn't just discard them as you do now. Eventually I became manageress of that shop and three others, and then it was sold up and I was out of work. This was in the 1920s when there was unemployment to the same extent as there is now (1980s). I think I wrote about eighty letters eventually. Didn't get a job that way. But I used to spend every morning walking round and going and asking for jobs, and if they said no I'd go again and again. I wouldn't take no for an answer. Eventually I got a job at Herrington's in their showrooms through sheer persistence. And then eventually I got a reply from Kirby & West, and I got a top job there. I stayed there twenty years. You've got to work at it, go and ask and ask! At Kirby & West I ran the wages office and the purchase office, and any complaints from the works all came through me to the bosses. And I enjoyed it. You'd got to prove you could do your job, and cope with any difficulties that arose.

Mona Lewis

Simpkin & James

I recollect quite well one or two sort of business people in other towns and cities who had sons. They would send them to Simpkin & James for training. It was often compared with Fortnum & Masons of London. I would say it was one of the surviving best class shops in the city of Leicester. My first job every morning was to scrub two steps on the Market Place side, and to clean all the brass lettering of the shop frontage, which took me from about half past eight in the morning to, say, half past nine. And this coincided with another errand boy, who did the Horsefair Street side, then both of us had to report to the Despatch Department, and we went out on a push bike with a carrier in front of it, which had a basket inside it, delivering small parcels all over the city and sometimes the country. They had delivery vans as well, but they went out with the bulk orders. These were small orders like the odd pound of cheese, or half a dozen cakes, or the odd carton of cream.

John Clarke

A sought-after position

Joseph Johnson's had what they called a hostel in Crescent Street for the unmarried staff. They used to live there, and the staff came up

Faire Brothers advertisement, 1911.

every lunchtime and had lunch at the hostel. At that time, going back years ago, to be a shop assistant was a very sought after position, and a lot of them didn't even get married.

Bridgit Lyons

The art of driving a tram

There was a big art in tram driving. You've heard them talk about Spaghetti Junction - well, it was like that on the Clock Tower with tram lines you know, going different routes, trams going to different places, some stopping, some coming back, and all that lark. Your first day on your own you wondered to yourself 'how the hell am I going to sort this lot out?'

You see, some of the points you had to go through were automatic, you had to use your brakes and your power to open them, and others opened and shut on their own. You had to learn all these. Of course it takes a little while, but you manage it in the end, after a lot of arguments and suchlike.

Mr A. Nicholls

Bone shakers

We used to call them bone-shakers. They were rattly, very rattly, and they were very cold in the winter – just wooden seats down each side. Upstairs there were wooden seats too. When you got to the terminus, the conductor or conductress had to change the trolley from one set of lines to the other to come back. You had a long pole, and you got the trolley with this pole off and put it on the line you needed to come back on, but my mate did mine for me, most of the time anyway. I did it once or twice, just to prove I could do it, but after that he would. Most of the chaps did it, anyway, where they'd got a woman conductor.

There were early starts. The earliest start was called five o'clock spare, and you had to be there at 5.20 a.m. To be spare meant you

Laying the lines before the introduction of electric trams in 1904.

Tram traffic around the Clock Tower.

were just there in case someone didn't turn up, drivers and conductors mixed in case someone was ill, as that tram had to go out at the proper time. That's how they covered it. Sometimes you were there so long it just got boring. We did buses and trams. Of course, on the bus you were spared all that changing the trolley business and that, and the buses were warmer, obviously. They were more enclosed. But the tram never got warm.

Blanche Harrison

Losing your duck

You're alright providing you keep your duck on – if you've got no duck, you've had it! It was like a wheel, not too big a wheel, but there was a groove in it that the wire used to run through. When you used to put the duck on the wire, you used to have a big long pole for it. You'd kind of stab it at it, you see. The trolley itself kept it tight, because there was tension on it, you see. But sometimes you'd

49

Leicester Prison staff in the 1920s. Mrs Howlett's father is third from the left in the second row.

get going along, or a tram had not switched over properly at the terminus, you come flying along and all of a sudden you're in darkness. Off comes your duck, beams going round up in the air, and down come the wires. You've had it. Then there's bad words. When your duck's off, you've had it, there's no doubt about that.

Mr A. Nicholls

Small change

We had a leather bag and a small change machine, by which I mean you could put shillings and sixpences, that was about all. That was for a quick change thing, but your coppers all went in your bag, which got heavy, so at the end, if you had time at the terminus, you would bag some of your money up, but you had to count it as you

put it in the bag – a little blue bag. Then at the end of the day, when you finished your shift, you went down to the offices and paid it in, and the cashier would count it all, and if you were short for any reason you had to make it up. The ticket number you started with had to tally with the number you finished with.

Blanche Harrison

Respect for the uniform

My father was a prison officer. People respected the uniform more than they do now. Of course, it was regular, and other people when they hadn't any work didn't have any dole at that time. When the prisoners were on remand, their families were allowed to bring in their dinner until they were sentenced, and I remember my father just getting his penknife and lifting up a bit of one dinner, and he found something had been hidden in this dinner.

I remember one of the officers kind of drilling them, you know, we could hear them. We could also hear them when they were in the chapel, and a favourite hymn of theirs was 'O God, Our Help in Ages Past'!

I remember seeing the Black Maria there, when there was a murder. They called it the Green Bicycle murder, and the man was there then, and he was taken to court, backwards and forwards in what was called the Black Maria which, when I saw it, had been painted up. It was brown, sort of two colours with a passage at the front and three or four doors on each side. I don't think there was hardly any room to sit down – but it was horse-drawn. There was a contractor who'd bring the horse when it was to be used, you see, to take the Black Maria out. There was also a little garage place for it.

Hilda Howlett

Looking after the park

What we did have to do in those days was all the swings. They used to be locked up then. We used to have to go first thing, unlock the parks, then unlock the swings. We had a routine and it was hard work. Our job was to make sure the toilets were cleaned out. There were three old age pensioners' huts where we used to have to go and light the fires, get them ready first thing, it took the first three hours, then we used to go on patrol and I used to come back down the Abbey Park and act as a park keeper. As a park keeper we used to go round and make sure there were no kids cycling – it was an offence to cycle in the park, there was 'Keep off the Grass' signs in the flower gardens. If there was anyone walking on the grass we used to tell them to get off, it was just general

patrolling and letting people know you were about, and people felt secure in those days.

A few years ago – I was a park ranger by this time – we had an influx of starlings, we were inundated. At the last count we had three million starlings swooping around the park because they were using it as a roost, and you wouldn't believe it but on the roads and the footpaths there was at least half an inch of droppings, and the park smelt terrible. They thought of some brilliant ways of getting rid of the starlings. We had a professor come along who suggested we put a loud speaker on top of the van, and we had a tape recording inside with the warning cry of starlings. So I was going round every night in the van, after the parks had closed, playing this tape. In the end the starlings took no notice and they just sat in the trees looking down at me. So the next idea was to get a cap pistol, a blank cap pistol. I went around, bang, bang, bang, and the starlings went flying from one branch to another. In the end they took no notice of that, so the final idea was bird scarers. There was a string of twelve bangers which went off every quarter of an hour right through the night, and we put out about twenty or thirty strings every night – so you can imagine bangers were going off in the park every few minutes. That was alright until the local people said 'we can't get to sleep', but first of all we had the police coming down the park saying 'there's people with shotguns on the park' – we forgot to inform them that we were going to set off bangers! So we had to time it so that we could only set them off between eight and ten at night, but you'd be surprised, the starlings got used to that and there was nothing that got them off. Eventually, after about two years, they found another roost, and I don't know if you remember but they went in the Town Hall Square then.

Dave Pick

Gardeners at Abbey Park in the 1920s.

Abbey Park.

Co-op funeral department

In 1948 I started in the funeral department. You started there to learn how to knock up coffins - they called it knocking up coffins. They were all ready-made. The Co-op had its own workshop to make coffins, but they also used to buy coffins ready-made from various people, you see. The coffins used to just come bare with a lid on. Now, by law, two inches of shavings must be in the bottom of the coffin to absorb any fluids, and at the top end where the head was going, they used to put a bunch of shavings and slope it up for the head to rest on. Then there used to be canvas, white canvas, placed on the bottom and tacked round the sides, so the whole of the inside of the coffin was in white canvas. Then there was a frill that went all the way around which was tacked on. The lid was lined as well. Before you put the shavings in and the lining, you'd drill the holes all the way round and fasten the handles on.

First of all they had some old Rolls Royces, enormous things they were, and they were special vehicles. One of these vehicles could be a car, or it could be a hearse, When it was used for a child's funeral, they got a glass case which held the child's coffin, and six people could sit in with the coffin in front of them. We used to call it the 'triple'.

Anonymous male contributor (2)

A career in archaeology

As a child growing up in the very early 60s, I became interested in history and anything old probably from the age of about four or five, mainly through visiting castles on holiday in Wales, that sort of thing, and also silly things like in those days your pocket money. You'd look at the heads on the coins, and you might find you'd got a coin of Queen Victoria from, I don't know, 1860 or something like that, and there'd be a real link with the past. It all developed from there really. It was visiting Jewry Wall Museum that sort of increased my interest in archaeology and made me channel my energies in that direction. When I was at school in the mid '70s, I managed to get the teachers on Wednesday afternoons to let me come and do a little bit of digging on sites in the city. I'd already had contact with the Senior Field Archaeologist – Jean Mellor – back in, oh it would be sometime in the early to mid '70s, and she just said 'well, come along to our excavations at the Austin Friars', the excavation of an Augustinian friary just by West Bridge, so I went there on Wednesday afternoons and occasionally on Sundays in about 1973/74, so that's how I got involved.

After the Austin Friars I then decided I needed to get a degree in archaeology if I wanted to carry on with a career in the subject, and so after 'A' levels I went up to the University of Durham and did a degree in archaeology there, and then also participated in some more excavation work. Like many archaeological graduates I sort of had to think 'well what am I going to do next?' I came back to Leicester and spoke to some of the people at the local unit here, and they said 'well we've got plenty of excavations running in Leicestershire', so I joined one on a temporary employment scheme back in the summer of '79, and I've been here ever since. The Norfolk Street villa excavation I worked on is one of the most exciting sites visually that's been done in the city for many, many years. Particularly exciting I think was when it was being machined and the JCB scraped virtually onto the top of a Roman tessellated pavement, which was nerve-wracking but exciting at the same time!

Richard Buckley

A religious vocation

When I actually entered, I was sixteen and a half. My family, well, I'd say they put nothing in the way, they didn't put any obstacles in the way. I think they saw it as the will of God, they felt I had a vocation and that was it.

We had rather strict rules. We wrote home once a month, and that letter was handed over open, and letters that we received were also open when we got them. In those years, when you left home, you left. That was my impression. I had a certain amount of difficulty in adjusting because I went in rather young, and secondly I'd been brought up in a big family – I imagine that really was the thing that made me find it difficult to live with a lot of women. We did a fair amount of work in the house. We had no lay Sisters. We were all equal and everybody had their turn. As a novice, we also instructed children, gave them Catechism classes on Sunday and Saturdays and different things like that. We also went out visiting, if a Sister was going out visiting they very often took one of us with them. And that was how my religious life began.

Anonymous female contributor (3)

Jewry Wall and the Roman baths, one of Leicester's most impressive Roman sites.

4 The First World War

Wounded soldiers returning to London Road railway station.

The outbreak of war

My earliest memory is the breaking out of the First World War on 4 August 1914. I recall a friend of mine, Johnny Smith and I, both seven years old, on our way to Aylestone equipped with home-made fishing net, jam jar and sandwiches, ruminating on the outbreak of war, and coming to the conclusion that it would be over by Christmas. My Dad volunteered and went to war, leaving Mother and five children to cope with wartime problems, which included the passing over of a zeppelin which scared the daylights out of us.

Albert Hall

Volunteering

Then came the war in 1914. I volunteered, I was one of the first hundred to volunteer, and then we paraded to Glen Parva. The first day we paraded in for our uniform, the second day we paraded. After the parade, the officer came up to me and said 'have you been in the army before, me boy?' I said 'no sir'. So he said 'where did you learn your drill?' I said 'the Church Lads Brigade', so he gave me a stripe! That was the first rung of the ladder. And then we went to Aldershot and took over the barracks there.

I had ten months training, and by God we did train! Unfortunately the recruits after that had three months training and out they went. I had a party of thirty men under me. They were all miners and they were marvellous men, all really marvellous men they were, comradely and brotherly. I was a corporal then, I had another stripe, but you never mixed with the men off parade. One gentleman, he lived in Wharf Street, and the

men went down to the pub at night, so I thought to myself 'where are they getting the money from?' So I did enquire, and one of the chaps, he bent irons round his neck, you know, the old iron fire irons, he used to bend them. So after that the hat went round the pub, and that's how they got the free beer.

After ten months training, in August 1915 we were sent out to France. There's this Constitutional Hill at Folkestone, all cobbled bricks, and in the dead of night, when it's pitch black and everything, the rhythm of your boots on this track, still brings it back - I went to France some years afterwards, and it all came back to me, walking down this hill. We arrived in France and after a few days at the base we went up the line. Oh dear, what an experience. I couldn't tell you exactly where, but we were only twenty-five yards from the Germans, and both the Germans and us had a tunnel underneath your road to blow each other up. But going down this tunnel you could hear the Germans, and we knew who was on the opposite side, whether they were Saxons or Prussians, because they were different types.

Herbert Weston

A terrible time

I remember the First World War vividly. I was four years old when it started. My oldest brother, who was twelve, came in and he said 'Come on, let's go and show you the gee gees'. We went to Mill Lane bridge and we sat on the parapet wall there and they were coming down from the Newarke. They stopped on the Boulevard for a while, then they got themselves together and they came round Mill Lane bridge, along the Eastern Boulevard, around Walnut Street to the sidings, where Berry's yard is, then by train to France.

I remember Hohenzollern Redoubt, which was a shocking thing for the local regiment.

Central engine shed, 1916. Women took on men's work during the war to release them for military service.

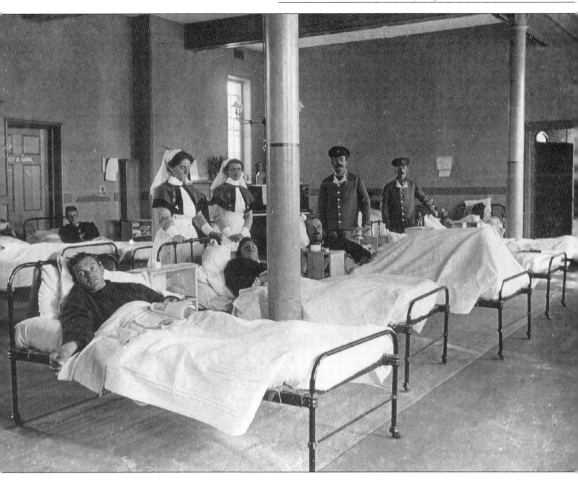

Ward at the North Evington Poor Law Infirmary, which became part of the Fifth Northern General Hospital during the war.

I always remember women running into each other's arms when the casualties were published. The Mercury man used to come round with a black edged border poster. Terrible time.

Mr G. Wells

Sleeping on the march

We walked everywhere, and we also travelled at night in the dark. We never travelled in the daytime because the enemy may see us. There were three nights of marching, but we rested during the day. The rhythm of your feet sent you to sleep marching, we did four miles per hour, then we had five minutes break. So of course when we gave a halt we were asleep, we were walking into the bloke in front, so the air was blue. Then we fell out for five minutes, and in again, and off we marched.

Herbert Weston

57

Temporary War Memorial in Town Hall Square.

The time of the gassing

We always had to go to church when we were youngsters, me and my young brother, I suppose he'd be perhaps eight during the war, and of course it was a semi-high church, St Mark's. We always put him at the end of the pew so's he could lay and close his eyes and go to sleep. Fast asleep. And it was a processional Sunday, so they comes down the aisle, you see, swinging the incense, and it just happened to be a good puff when it got to the end of our pew, and he woke up and said 'Good God, I'm gassed!'. It was the time of the gassing, you know. Oh dear, we didn't know what to do with him!

Mrs Walton

In the trenches

We did four days and four nights in the trenches. Well, it was appalling. There was four inches of water, which we waded in for four days and four nights, and it was terribly cold. We were frost bitten, so to speak, but in the evening about 11 o'clock, a canteen of tea came up, and there was rum inside and it gave us new life. Well, we WERE alive, and we weren't, so to speak. But it was appalling. I can't describe it really.

But we came out of the trenches into the billet. We were wet through and we took our

Opposite: Imports were severely affected by German U-boat action from 1917.

socks off, and my feet were wizened up with the frostbite. But I was lucky again, because some of my friends took their socks off, and some of the toes came off with them. It was appalling, and they were shipped to hospital at once, but you can't describe it really. The enemy was there, admittedly, but of course we'd got no thought of them, we'd got to look after ourselves. We were tough, we must have been tough, well we WERE tough, but that was that.

Herbert Weston

Meagre rations

There was the day to day pursuit of food during the First World War. Being the eldest,

I was the main purveyor, up at 5 a.m., joining queues at shops, particularly Folwell's, and Walkers butchers in the Market Place in winter and summer. I had a note from Mum to take to school when I was late, explaining the reasons. There were occasional rumours of stocks of Australian tinned jam, which required a lightning visit to possible venues. I remember I used to go out after school and go chasing up all sorts of places as far as Charnwood Street, because somebody had told my Mother that they were selling jam. Saturday mornings when Mother was at work, I started queuing up outside Parker's the butchers in Belgrave Gate for our meat ration. Sometimes we were unlucky as stocks were sold out. I remember one Saturday when the

Queuing for food in the Market Place.

Armistice Day speech outside the Town Hall by the Mayor, Alderman W. Lovell.

Frisby's collector for the weekly payment of one shilling to purchase boots and shoes brought us half a frozen rabbit, Australian. We were delighted for it was an addition to our meagre rations. I always remembered when Dad came home on leave, not very often, he was in France. He had special extra food allowances, and being a soldier was dealt with generously by shopkeepers.

Albert Hall

She thought it was cat

We made do mostly with vegetables and what meat we could get, and I do remember once that my father had acquired a rabbit and my mother, when she cooked it, refused to have any because she said she didn't think it was a rabbit, she thought it was cat. It could have been possibly.

Mr G. Wells

Taken prisoner

In June 1916 the Germans had been bombarding our barbed wire, so an officer, myself and a private went out to repair it. I got hit then, a bullet through my arm. It paralysed me. I was surprised, I was sent down to the base. I lost the use of my arm for six months, but after treatment it came back. And that was that. Then I reported to the Third Battalion Leicestershire Regiment, and there I was instructing for eighteen months.

Unveiling of the permanent War Memorial in Victoria Park in 1925.

In March 1918 I went back to France, and I didn't know any of the platoon, so they didn't know me, then the Germans were attacking again, so we went up the front line. The Germans were dropping shells all round us, and they were dropping THIS way, so I said to the platoon 'for God's sake, when they drop one in there, run like hell!' I was in the centre of them, I got through, but some of the boys on the left didn't. But then I had an order to retreat. Well, before that, the Colonel came up and he said 'what the Hell are you doing here? I ordered you to go to the base camp for a commission – what are you going to do?' I says 'I'll stay with the boys'. But then I had the order to retire, which we

did, but the Germans were waiting for us, they broke through on our right, they were waiting for us, you see. So that was that.

I was taken prisoner of war in a French camp which was loused up. There were about thirty of us in a cell, loused up, we were. But we got transferred to Geissen, which was a permanent prisoner-of-war camp, and on arrival there they gave us a parcel, a food parcel, and after that my parents paid to St John's (Ambulance) and I had, I think, six parcels come out to me, and they were marvellous parcels. But the biscuits were hard, so we pierced a hole through, and we put them underneath the tap which swelled them. Then we put them in the sun, and we had new bread! I spent six months as a prisoner. An experience. And then I came home.

Herbert Weston

Everywhere was blacked out, every porthole was screwed down, so in the terrific heat you literally sweated it out.

Mona Lewis

Stranded in Australia

My brother had emigrated to Australia, and Mother and I badly wanted to go and visit him. Well, father was getting on well in business in those days, so we could afford to go. It took us six weeks to get there, and of course there was no air conditioning on the ship, so when we came to the Red Sea, oh dear, we were just cooked in an oven! Well, we'd been in Australia just three weeks when the First World War started, so we were stuck out there for three years. We desperately wanted to get home, but there were no passenger ships in those days. But by a fluke, we managed to get two passenger berths on an old P&O, 9, 000, ton liner that was due to be broken up when it got back to England. It took us nine weeks to get home – we had to zig-zag all the way because of submarines. And of course the male passengers took it in turns to watch day and night, and we slept in our life belts. We had little hard straw mattresses, with bugs in the bed. It was absolute hell, that boat. And you could see, as the boat tipped if you were in a swell, that the ceiling parted slightly from the walls.

Armistice Day

I remember on Armistice Day I went out early with a man on his horse and cart which belonged to a dairy in Wharf Street, and he went out to their farm at Knighton. On the way back we heard about the Armistice being carried out, and he promptly left me with the horse and cart and went into the nearest pub, and by the time he came out he was drunk and I had to accept responsibility for coming home.

Albert Hall

We're all friends now

I was in Mesopotamia, and I shall never forget it, we were going across the river in a small boat. I remember going on shore and somebody challenged me. I says 'Friend! we're all friends now!' Most of the chaps thought that'd be the war to end all wars, but we know now that the world's in more turmoil now than at almost any period in history apart from the actual warfares.

Mr Walton

5 Political Campaigns

March of Unemployed Men from Leicester to London in 1905.

March of unemployed men

I was twelve at the time of the march of unemployed men to London in 1905. The Education people stepped in and stopped me from marching to London with my father. I went to Market Harborough with him, but the police must have got to know about it, and of course they started to sort me out. I tried to get away with it, trying to hide where I possibly could, but they picked me up at the

finish, and one of the fellows belonging to the march was asked to take me back to Leicester, down to the Midland station, and I walked from the Midland station half with me shoes off. I got very footsore!

Both my sisters worked at Butler's in Walnut Street, and they were sacked because they went to the trade union meeting. They wasn't trade unionists, you see, they were sacked just for going to the meeting. My sisters were asked to speak at a meeting in the

Market Place by Jabez Chaplin. He took the case up over my sisters being stopped, and they both went up on the platform at Leicester Market.

George White

Campaigning for the tenants

My activity of a political nature started with the Braunstone Tenants' Association because we had to take political action to deal with the many problems which affected the tenants on that estate. In fact, we were part of a number of tenants' associations throughout the whole of the country who formed the National Council of Tenants' Associations, of which our Secretary was the Secretary, and I was a member of the Executive Committee. We put pressure on the government to try and change their policies in regard to the present and future housing, Council housing activities and developments. Most of the people in the Association were active in their trade unions, and it was inevitable and natural that they should take action as far as their housing and environment was concerned. All the railwaymen, particularly the Great Central Railway, were well organized, and they were very prominent both in local authority representation, and also very militant in relation to their conditions of employment, and the organization of the National Union of Railwaymen.

I personally started to get some education in respect to the working class history of this country, and my first lessons took place in the National Council of Labour College's classes which were mainly held in the Secular Hall in Humberstone Gate. I became very active in my trade union and represented my branch at the Trades Council, and also got elected to the District Committee of the union. I became very

active to improve the economic, social and environment conditions of ordinary people. Our Council house front room became the meeting place of the Labour Party and acted as headquarters for the elections, both local and national. This led me to all sorts of other activities.

Albert Hall

Joining the British Union of Fascists

I wrote to the Blackshirt headquarters in King's Road, Chelsea, commonly called the Barracks. I went down on a five shilling trip and joined at the place, paying a shilling. And I came back, as far as I know, the first one in Leicester. This was October 1933. There used to run in Leicester a Leicester Parliamentary Debating Society, and it used to meet in the schoolroom in Colton Street. It ran on exactly the same procedures as the House of Commons. They had a Speaker, a party in power – it was changed from year to year – and therefore a Prime Minister, and Leader of the Opposition. And they would draw up parliamentary Bills, proper printed Bills to put before the House, and the debates went on as an exercise in parliamentary democracy and discussion. Of course, I turned up as the first fascist member for Chelsea. I think it faded out in the war years and has never been revised, but that was one of the recognised societies of Leicester and brought together all the political leaders in Leicester of different persuasions. It was a very fine thing.

We formed a Leicester branch and the activities gradually spread. We tried to get headquarters in each constituency, usually a street corner shop which we rented for about ten bob a week. We began organizing a series of public meetings, and organizing the elections. Of course, I used to write letters to

Ramsay MacDonald, MP for Leicester 1906-1918, campaigning in the Market Place.

the Mercury and exaggerate things. When they used to attack us, it was obviously policy to play on our great strength, but I would think we were getting up to four or five hundred members. That includes the group of active members, the Blackshirts, we used to wear the uniform until it was banned in 1936, we'd hold the public meetings, we'd go out and help steward in the Midland region. That was great fun, going out, and we even in the summer would go out to the villages like Tugby, and I remember going to Ratby and places and had meetings there. Oakham, we had Oswald Mosley at Oakham. And we had three quite strong branches, we must have had 150 in each, men and women. The women were particularly keen and active. But that would include a number of unrecorded

businessmen, obviously for security reasons, who used to pay subscriptions but we didn't classify their names.

W. Gough

Working men's university

I've got a picture where I was addressing 2,000 people when Mosley was having a meeting down at the Junior Training Hall (Granby Halls). They were bashing them about down there, you know. It's a wonder he didn't become the leader of the Labour Party – he was in it at one time. The Market Place used to be a sort of working men's university on Sunday morning. They could all go and join in. One of the Conservatives, Charlie

Pearce, he was speaking in the Market Place one day, and the chaps got hold of the shafts of the trap, ran him into London Road, and pelted him with oranges.

Mr Walton

Holding forth in the Market Place

When we started in 1934 in the Market Place, Sunday night was an open forum for various religious cranks and Communists and various left-wing organizations, then we started. You had the old trestle stalls. You'd just stand on one and hold forth. You'd got a ready made audience of three or four hundred, and general hostility, you see, and we began to get a bit of rough stuff. I can remember being young and uneducated in these matters. I hurled abuse at them once, accusing them of being a lot of yellow rats! But after that, there was a ban, you see. No more Blackshirt meetings in the Market because they were getting disruptive, and they gave us this site in Humberstone Gate where the Weighbridge was. Outside there was the horse trough, and the trams used to come by within a few feet. We built that up, a regular Sunday night meeting, which had very, very little opposition.

W. Gough

Keeping low about it

I didn't join as a member of the Communist Party until 1935. I had to keep very low about it indeed, because of the pressure on teachers at the Wyggeston Girls. We had to tread very carefully. I used to go a lot in the early days to Women's Institutes and meetings of that kind, to factory meetings, and I used to talk about Russia, Soviet Russia. I didn't do it on behalf of the Party. I was always at one side, a

bit like a fellow traveller as far as the Party was concerned. It grew with the advent of the Left Book Club, but it was never a very powerful party.

D. Adams

Spanish Civil War

We lost three comrades from Leicester: Roy Watts, Fred Sykes and another. We formed a Spanish Aid Committee with Victor Lenthall as Secretary and myself, Albert Hall, as Chairman. There was also a Basque Children's Refugee Committee, to which Mrs Attenborough was actively associated. The Spanish Aid Committee was assisted in its activities by young Richard, now Sir Richard Attenborough. Collections were on Sunday mornings, sometimes by car and sometimes by handcart. There was never any connection between the Spanish Aid Committee (to support the Republican cause) and the Basque Children's Committee. As I say, they were mainly benevolent middle class people, and there was no sort of link-up at all.

Albert Hall

Alcatraz House

Our sympathy to the Franco regime is perhaps exemplified by what we called our new headquarters in Upper Wellington Street - the Alcatraz House - which of course was the castle in which Franco's men heroically held out against the Communists for nearly eighteen months. But of course the slight effect of the war was that the Communist element in Leicester was much more anti-Fascist at that time, but the general opinion was that the public in general had not the slightest interest in what was going on in Spain. However much you

Suffragette meeting in the Market Place in the early twentieth century.

tried to whip up enthusiasm, they were more concerned about domestic problems. We had an influx of refugees into Leicester from the Basque territory, to which we strongly objected in our lack of wisdom of those times, realising the refugee problems of latter years, because we felt there were enough English boys and girls in a state of poverty that deserved our attention, rather than these children being driven out of Basque territory.

W. Gough

Opposing the war

From 1937 onwards, as the approach to war seemed to become inevitable, public support waned and hostile opposition toward us was more sustained. It was left more to the hardcore to try and work on the thesis that we were building a political party capable of governing the country and keeping the country out of war. Right up to August 1939, my last public meeting was at the dockyard gates in Portsmouth, of all places, speaking to the dockyard workers. I've still got a piece of the platform now, inscribed, smashed to pieces! But we tried as hard as we could to keep Britain out of war. In hindsight, of course, you've probably got different opinions and different views, but our chief problem, the reason why we were so keen, was we realised that Britain hadn't the capacity to fight a war, within the situation of disarmament. So there didn't seem much hope if we did go to war.

W. Gough

First lesson in politics

My first lesson in politics was when I was eleven, at the Gateway College. We were told that because we'd all got the suit, we'd all got a uniform which was exactly the same, that made us all equal you see. But the fact was that my uniform was on a ticket from the Co-op, because we were only ordinary poor people, and it was made of barathea, and when it rained the sleeves extended by about four inches on my uniform, but on the other people's uniforms, they were gabardine, and the rain went bouncing off them, you see! So just because you'd got a uniform which looks the same, it doesn't really mean to say that you're equal! So that was a big lesson to me, and I was determined at the time to beat these other people at everything.

I was made aware of the Communist Party by one of the comrades. He joined, and he let me know about it. For a time I didn't join, because I was busy doing other things. The only time they used to have a meeting was on Sunday nights, and I was invariably doing something else, you know, because the progressive movement does a lot of work at the weekends, and I was going down to London and one thing and another. So what I had to do then was kind of pick and choose, when I'd got the time, and then see what was on at the Secular Hall. It was always seen by me as a centre for the kind of debate that you couldn't get anywhere else. But it was also quite varied. We're a bit bloody-minded, but that's how it happens, you see, because otherwise there's no debate, if no one is playing Devil's advocate.

Our party is about the emancipation of people. The fact that it's been tried in other countries, though never been successful yet, whereas human beings, we only learn by the mistakes that we make, so it was never going to be an instant success.

Colin Green

Early twentieth-century sketch of the Secular Hall in Humberstone Gate.

6 Housing and Health

Denmark Street, in the Wharf Street area of Leicester.

Desperately overcrowded

We lived in a small four roomed house in Fleet Street Terrace, which of course has been demolished for many, many years now. Two were bedrooms, one the front bedroom (about nine foot six by five foot) and one small bedroom (about eight foot by four foot six). We were desperately overcrowded. I well remember that we had concrete floors and we were not very warm, but we survived. We had

two lavatories in the back yard which covered eight houses, and there was always conflict about the state in which they were left.

Albert Hall

Radio Times

We used to have the Radio Times. Times were hard then, and it might seem a bit of an extravagance to spend twopence on a Radio

Times, but it had another use as well because when it finished on a Saturday, on the Sunday it was ripped into four and threaded on a bit of string, and that was the loo paper. No luxuries like Andrex!

Mr R. Issitt

Bath night

People washed in the kitchen, and from the pump if they were lucky enough to have a pump. No hot water, of course, they had to boil it on the fire. The tin baths used to hang outside on a nail. They used to fetch them in on Friday night, and everybody had a bath. But it was a case of filling the kettles up, you see, to get hot water to have a bath. That went on for years. I mean, when I was at home, we had a zinc bath. There were six of us, you see, I was the youngest, and this is what we had to do. But emptying the thing down the sink was the biggest nuisance, to get on with the next one!

Mrs G. Matthews

Poverty stricken

I remember I used to pass the slaughterhouse when I went to school at Christow Street, I think it was on the corner of Carley Street and Brunswick Street. Many a time I've seen them bringing the sheep down for slaughter, and they all used to herd into the yard at the back of houses as well. It was rough, yes. I mean, I had friends who lived further down Wharf Street and they were really poverty-stricken. You'd go in their houses and it was just the bare bricks on the floors, and newspaper on the tables, and I've been in and there's been fowls pecking about in the room. The tap was in the yard for them, but it was a way of life for them. But yes, Wharf Street did have a name for being rough.

Iris Smith

Pentonville

One went down Bonners Lane and turned left into Grange Lane and the first entrance on the left was Pentonville. Now you went in through an open gateway and what fronted you were about four or five houses on the left and about four facing you, and down the other side I have an idea there was a toilet block. There was a woman there who had two kids. I went in there one morning in the late winter, and she said 'my roof's leaking'. She opened the front bedroom door and walked over to the far corner of the room and said 'there it is, you can see it's very wet indeed'. As I turned to go out I looked round the walls and there were long red streaks coming down all the walls, so I said 'have the kids been trying to do some decoration?'. She said 'what do you mean?' I said 'all the streaks down the wall'. 'Oh', she said, 'the kids have to kill the bugs every night before they get into bed'.

Mr Tom Crosher

Washday

Always on a Monday, in an old copper in the kitchen. The fire was lit and the whites were all boiled in that, and the old tub, and the old mangle. Oh yes, and the dolly tub, I've used the lot. It's quite nice to see them when I go round anywhere, but yes, that was a big day. On that day we always had cold meat if there was any left, and mashed potatoes, or something, a makeshift in other words for dinner because Mum was so busy.

Blanche Harrison

Black leading

There were the old fireplaces in the kitchen where there was an oven to cook with, and on the other side there was a big boiler where the water was heated from the fire. First thing in the morning, you had your tin of black lead and your black lead brush. You spread this all over these hobs and grates, and you'd polish away with another brush. After that you polished it all with a velvet duster, until you were as black as the grate when you'd finished. And then of course there was all the ashes to get up, and the coal. You went to the coal house and smashed up these great lumps of coal, then you carried heavy buckets of coal in. That was the first day's job. Life for a housewife was just hard work from morning till night.

Mona Lewis

Electricity!

Some houses didn't even have a gas mantle, they had the bare gas pipe, very, very dangerous - the gas just shooting out. Until one day, of course, progress, and electricity was put into the houses. That was wonderful. The very fact that you could just hit a little switch on the wall and get wonderful light. Brilliant!

Mr G. Stacey

No carpets

In those days, no one had a carpet as such, not as we know it today, wall to wall. It was mostly mats, and once or twice a week they were taken up, shook, hung on the line, then we'd go round with a mop, or mostly on knees, and wash the floor properly all over. But my grandma did have a carpet in the dining room. She had a house where there was a scullery, a kitchen cum living room, and a big dining room,

Tudor Road. Unlike housing built before the 1870s, these were regulated by local bye-laws.

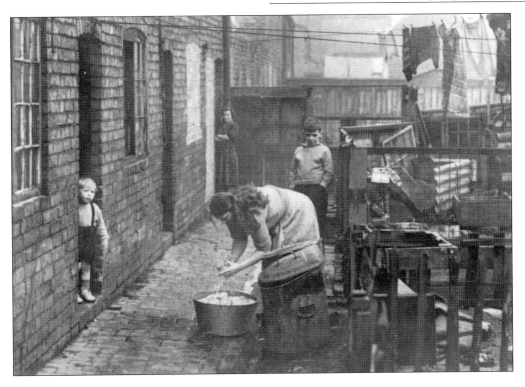

Housing conditions in Leicester between the wars.

and then a parlour. And there was the hall. She was in a different kind of house to the one we were. Although she was in the same street, Buller Street, it was a large house and she had a scullery, and she had a carpet sweeper which she bought through a club like the Great Universal. These clubs, they were a shilling a week thing, you could have what you want. They have catalogues in other words, you see, and Grandma was never one for going into debt, but she would have something from this club. A friend of hers ran this club, a neighbour, and she would have one article and get it paid for before she would buy anything else. But she got the carpet sweeper. It was an old Ewbank, I recall it as being old and made of wood.

Blanche Harrison

Pegging a rug

You never had a carpet in those days, you'd probably sit and peg a rug. Get a lump of sacking from the local shops or whatever, and sit and cut. You never threw clothes away, just cut them up and made a rug out of them. They were devils to get clean, so I used to hang them on the line, or shake them really hard, because all the bits used to get through. They were really warm.

Jackie Harvey

Spring cleaning

In the old days there were no modern appliances. No hoovers, no washing machines. Spring cleaning time was sheer hell for a week or a fortnight. The carpets were all taken up, they were dragged out, flung across the line, you had a carpet beater and you beat the hell out of them. Then you stood in a cloud of thick dust that had accumulated all the year, because there were no hoovers to suck it out. Every inch of paint in the house was washed, every drawer turned out, everything polished, and at last you could sit down with a sigh of relief. Your house had been cleaned through.

Mona Lewis

Living in the Prison

After the war my father came back and went to Leicester Prison, and he was there for nearly three years. He couldn't get a house anywhere, so he got permission from the Home Office to use the house that was inside the prison where the female officers were, because at one time there was just that part used for female prisoners. We were there for three years. It was quite good. Two rooms downstairs, and three bedrooms and a bathroom. Stone floors. There was a little exercise yard and a laundry the other side. The men used to come across and use the laundry, but we had permission to use it every Thursday.

We had to go through the main gate, but there was a little door. We had to be in by ten o'clock because the gates were locked up then, and if there had been anything, anybody taken ill or anything, there was a key in a glass case which had to be broken to open the gate, and then a whole list, the whys and wherefores, had to be written down and sent to the Home Office about what had happened. Many a time I've had to run down Welford Road to get in, and one night he'd

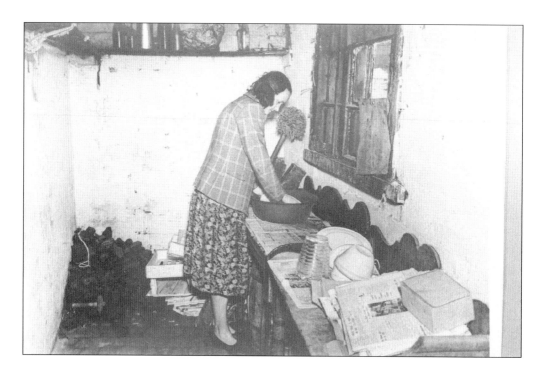

In the kitchen.

Pochin's 'Servall' cooker and grate – undreamed of luxury in working-class homes.

[the Chief Officer] just locked up, and I was locked out, and my father came to the iron gate and told the gate officer there to tell me to go down to my grandfather's for the night, and I'd got my brother with me, so we had to stay there that night. Once he locked up, you're locked in or out! The prison governor lived in the big house at the side, and he had no access from his house to the inside. He had to come through the main gates every time.

We had a little bit of garden. It was quite OK, but we didn't go about the prison – only just in our own little vicinity. Because it had been quite a privilege to live there, my father was rather strict that we kept to our part. If I mentioned that I lived in the prison, I detected that people were a bit sceptical about it! It was a big concession to go and live there. I took it to be just ordinary. It was home. Home is where your furniture and your

things are, isn't it? Rather grey and dark, the stonework, you know, if you look at it like that. But it was alright when we were inside, you didn't mind. We were together, you see, because my mother had been waiting to come down all those years.

Mrs Hilda Howlett

... and in the wilderness!

We finally got permission to go live at the Braunstone estate. I think one of the primary considerations by the Housing Committee was the fact that I was a skilled woodworker and they anticipated that I would be able to afford to pay the rents, which were fairly high in those days, comparatively high. But the conditions on the Braunstone estate were such that we formed a Tenants' Association, as there was no made up road,

Leicester Prison.

no transport, no shops, no schools, and it was just like living in houses in the wilderness. We formed the housing association and started to raise problems, raise organizations to deal with the situation, and the people we first attacked was the Housing Committee for the high rents, and then the rest of the City Council, at that time, in relation to the absence of made up roads, no buses, no schools, no shops, as we were completely isolated. The nearest we could go by local transport to the Braunstone estate was at the bottom of the Western Park, or if we had been shopping, as we had to do in the town or on the way, it meant carrying our stuff up the Shoulder of Mutton hill right onto the estate, or if you came the other way, they had

to come from Narborough Road onto the estate, and this of course created a good many problems.

I remember that we were very busy organizing the tenants on the Western Park side of the estate, and we used to charge two shillings a year and we used to collect it at sixpence a quarter, and I remember that I used to go out collecting the sixpence a quarter for their subscription most Sunday mornings, and then often we got all the problems which they were concerned with, so that we had to try and do our best to eliminate many of the hardships that were being created by the failure of the local authority and the government at that time to give any consideration to the environment in which we were living.

The activities of the Tenants' Association in the first place were very limited, and most of them took place in our front room on Winstanley Drive, but when we were successful in getting schools built we were then able to hire rooms, and we had a number of committees which included a Gardening Committee, which was responsible for the annual garden competition for which they received cups and cash, which helped considerably to maintain the estates. And we had an Ambulance Committee; a St. John Ambulance Committee. We also held whist drives and dances, and of course our main preoccupation was the problem of rents and the environment on the estate, for which the main committee used to be largely concerned with.

Albert Hall

Elite types of houses

But ultimately, as a result of our organization, we did manage to get the Council to accept their responsibilities over a number of years, and we maintained our organization to deal with all sorts of problems, particularly including rent increases right until the commencement of the Second World War. There were difficulties in paying the rent, but of course the ordinary working people at that time, their characters were such that they hated to be in debt for anyone, and they struggled to pay the rent, which was always number one priority, because if they didn't pay it, the prospects were that they would be evicted.

As far as the houses themselves were concerned, although there was no luxury about them, by the conditions that operated in housing generally at that time, we felt we were in rather elite types of houses, and of course we had gardens, and as was the

philosophy of the working people in those days, they took a great deal of pride in maintaining both the houses and the gardens, and we were very proud of them because they were far in advance of most of the houses that we had been living in, and been born and bred in, so that we did appreciate the improvements that had taken place. But by present day standards of course, they were rather backward, and the housing association did press the Housing Committee of the local Council to institute better arrangements for heating the water in the bathroom than what we had at that time, which was a pump in the kitchen in which the water was heated by gas in the tub, and then we pumped it upstairs, pumped it through up into the bathroom, and in many cases pumps broke down and lots of the people had to carry the hot water up in buckets to put it in the bath.

Albert Hall

Collecting the rent

I became a rent collector, and I collected on almost all the estates in Leicester. There must be thousands of people who know me! At Braunstone they used to pay 5s and a halfpenny for the bungalows in Woodshawe Rise. The parlour houses were 8s 11d. One chap, he was behind, and I said 'well, what about these arrears?'. He says, 'well, I reckon I'm keeping you in a job!'. I says, 'you've got to clear these arrears. The other people are keeping you in this house'. It was a very poor area.

Mr Walton

Inside toilets

The houses on Saffron Lane were much better. I mean, they'd lived in a house and shared. It was a row of terraced houses with shared loos, outside loos. And although the toilets on Boulder Lane were actually in the porch, at least there were toilets there, and I mean, when my mother moved down to Melland Place, the toilets were inside. You didn't get any hot water. You had to pump the hot water up with the copper being on, and that took about half an hour to get it boiled up. I can tell you what, it's a wonder that my skin's survived. I can remember my mother doing the washing, and then pumping the washing water into the bath, and they'd have a bath in it. She couldn't afford to heat the water twice.

There were grates in both bedrooms, and yet oddly enough there wasn't one in the small room, the box-room, and yet that was always the coldest and dampest room. They were those little metal fireplaces with the little grates in, they cost a fortune now. They sell them to the antiques centres. Of course, we had lino down, and the quarry tiles in the halls and passageways. There were certain things you couldn't do, like knocking walls out, which one or two people did because they wanted a through lounge. So people knocked the walls out and wouldn't let the rent man in, so that he couldn't see what you'd done!

Interwar municipal housing was regarded as 'elite' by comparison with slum areas such as this.

North Braunstone Estate, built in the 1930s as part of the slum clearance programme.

Because we always used to have the rent man come, and I always remember, when you hadn't any money, my mum used to say 'Go and tell him that I'm not in', you know.

Jackie Harvey

The houses in between

New Parks was fields until after the war. My husband lived on Liberty Road before we were married, and from his garden you could see the War Memorial and De Montfort Hall, because Leicester's in a dip, you see, and you rise to come here. And to stand on the bay windows you could see Old John that side. Well, when we built this house in 1952/53, we didn't realise until we'd gone upstairs that

Large gardens were also a feature of 1920s and 1930s Council housing.

you couldn't see anything, 'cos we thought 'oh well, we'll be able to see all Leicester!'. But you can't because of the semi-detached houses they built. All at the bottom here was cornfields, and then of course the railway further over where it cuts through. On the Braunstone Frith and New Parks, the roads were all laid out before the houses were built, by the Italian prisoners of war.

Marjorie Smart

Silver buttons

My brother worked for Dr McAllister-Hewlings in the Spa in Humberstone Gate. He left at fourteen. I was twelve, and I took it over, wearing silver buttons and long trousers, and I got four shillings a week for taking private medicine out in neatly wrapped bottles in white paper, red seal, and the address, and also letting the private patients in. Now he had a coachman, a dispenser who was also his sister, and he had an Airedale dog running under the axle of the trap which he used to go to the patients. A very smart man.

Mr S. Coleman

Live or die

Typhoid fever, smallpox, chicken pox, TB – they were the most difficult diseases. There were not the drugs. Now, I'm going back thirty years now, when I was a grown woman, and I contacted a TB kidney. Well, luckily, streptomycin had just been used, and I was able to be cured, but the streptomycin damaged the nerves on one side. I understand that streptomycin now is very, very different, but until streptomycin I think you had to, if you were lucky, go to Switzerland or some cold place where it was literally frozen out of you. So these days there's a lot to be thankful

Tuberculosis wards at Groby Road Isolation Hospital.

for where illness is concerned. You just had to live through it and either live or die.

Mona Lewis

No medicinal treatment

There was no medicinal treatment to which the TB bug was susceptible. Treatment fifty years ago was rest, fresh air, good food, and if you could afford it, residence for several months in the special sanatoria, usually at high altitudes, with plenty of sun.

Dr M. Millard

Yellow cards

There was a lot of TB. The bottom end of Belgrave, there was one really very nice area, big houses, but most of them had TB people, and it was easier for us going from perhaps one to the other than distance, 'cos we went on our bikes, you see, there were no motor cars then. But TB always bothered us, from nursing people that were dying of TB then, to the surgical side where there were children as well as grown ups which we hoped to get better. As I say, an infection would have gone through the whole family, but the doctors stepped in and made them have tests even then. They were covered by some sort of health service that was going through the workplaces. They had to pay a halfpenny a week, which covered the whole family, which was a marvellous idea, because we could get right down to it. When we went in and found somebody ill, and they'd say 'will you look at the little girl', and we had to say 'have you got a yellow card?'. And we had to check up on the yellow cards.

Mrs G. Matthews

...and green ones

Now in Chester Street was the Leicester Public Medical Service, which was always called 'the Clinic', opposite St. Matthew's church. And there was free medical attention for everybody, especially children, much patronised by the schoolchildren. They all had clinic cards, a green clinic card they'd carry with them, so if they had a scab on them, or they cut themselves, or anything, or they weren't well, you sent them round the Clinic to see Nurse Burden, and she was there for years and years and years.

Margaret Zientek

Very neighbourly

They were very neighbourly. I mean, you could get anything from a neighbour. Many, many times I've called through the kitchen window and said 'Mrs Smith, can you give me something for the old lady. She's not very comfortable and I haven't got a drawsheet or anything'. And she'd say 'half a minute, Nurse. I'll find you a bit of the old man's shirt!'. But we managed. It was such a happy atmosphere. You never got anybody refuse, and they'd say 'Oh, I'll come in, Nurse, and give them a drink of tea before you come again', or 'I'll keep an eye on them, and I'll let our Willie run down if she's worse'. You see, we had no communication, we'd no telephones, no way of getting help if we needed it.

Mrs G. Matthews

Sheer bedside nursing

We just nursed them. If a patient came in with pneumonia, and quite a lot did in those days, then it was sheer bedside nursing. And if they went into crisis with a high temperature, they would be tepid bathed in bed. The round of pressure points, of course, was three times a day. The trolley was always made up, and you rubbed their bottoms with soap and water until it went in, and then you finished off with methylated spirits and a thin dusting of talcum powder. And that was done three times a day. We never had bedsores. We were in Matron's office if anybody got a bedsore. The City General was a rate-aided hospital, of course, and so people were means tested. They paid what they could afford towards their treatment. But one thing that was drilled into us was the best use of materials. You had to be careful about everything, a piece of lint, or a piece of cotton wool. Every time you broke a thermometer, down to Matron's office. I was amazed when I went down recently to the Royal Infirmary to find that they're disposable now!

Pat Russell

Black boards and straw

Back in the old days when anyone was very, very ill or on the point of death, it was quite common for straw to be laid out on the streets to deaden the noise of traffic passing by, horses hooves and the rattle of carts and motor vehicles, and usually a black board used to be taken and screwed under the front window, a long black board screwed from the bottom to the top of the window to indicate to passers by and people in the streets that there'd been a death in that house.

Anonymous male contributor (2)

Home deliveries

Most of the deliveries were home deliveries, because it cost money to go in the hospital then. I think, really, it was a guinea then to

Staff of the North Evington Poor Law Infirmary in the late 1920s. The Infirmary became Leicester General Hospital in 1930.

go into the hospital and be looked after. But then, you see, if you've got a whole lot of children, who's going to mind the children while you're in hospital? And they never liked the idea. They liked the idea of being at home with the family, so that when the baby was born everything was happy. But they had a lot of faith in the midwife. They had large families because there was no contraception. I remember clearly Dr Porteous – he was on Humberstone Road then – he would give the father such a wigging. He told him she wasn't to have any more children, it was dangerous. This was before she had the eleventh, but he never told him what to do!

Mrs G. Matthews

Your babies came

Of course, there was no birth control. Your babies came, and you said that happens, nothing you could do about it. They just took nature as it was handed out to them. And when you were pregnant, well, if you were a bit sensitive, you just did not go out, you didn't like people to see you. And when the babies were born – they were mostly born at home – and if it was a difficult birth, anaesthetic was very crude, and often the birth was a birth by what they used to term the instruments.

Mona Lewis

Annual Nurses' service at Leicester Cathedral in the late 1930s.

Fighting for birth control

Marie Stopes, in the mid-50s I think it was, talked at the Secular Hall about her fight for birth control. She did a lot of sterling work, and she even persuaded the Church of England that it was a good idea from about 1930 onwards. She was a bit paranoid about the Roman Catholics though. She imagined there was one hiding behind every lamp post plotting against her, you know towards the end. She sounded really as if she'd joined the Conservative Party at the time when she came down to the Secular, and she upset one or two of the audience when she said that the lower class people had too many children. They were the ones that should have birth control, you see, and furthermore, if they didn't agree to have birth control they shouldn't get any public assistance or anything like that. So one lady got up and told her she ought to be ashamed of herself and walked out!

Harold Hammersley

Half-cooked liver

I went to Harrison Road School, but unfortunately the year I should have taken the scholarship I had very bad anaemia, and I was kept away from school for about six months. I was told to go out in the fresh air, you know, do a bit of gardening or whatever, but the doctor wouldn't let me go to school. My mother was told to give me plenty of liver, half cooked, and a glass of milk with a glass of sherry in it, I think. Things like that, home remedies, you know.

Blanche Harrison

Brimstone and treacle

In the spring, if you were itching, or when they used to say 'oh, it's your blood overheating', Mother always used to give us brimstone and treacle, or brimstone and jam, which we loathed! Oh, we thought it was horrible! And then if you'd got a cold or a cough, they used to rub goose grease on your chest and on your back, and cover it with brown paper - and they always said that was exceptionally good. And another thing, for eczema, was equal parts of pure lard and boracic powder, mixed into a paste and

Large families were common, but infant and maternal welfare services helped to reduce previously high death rates.

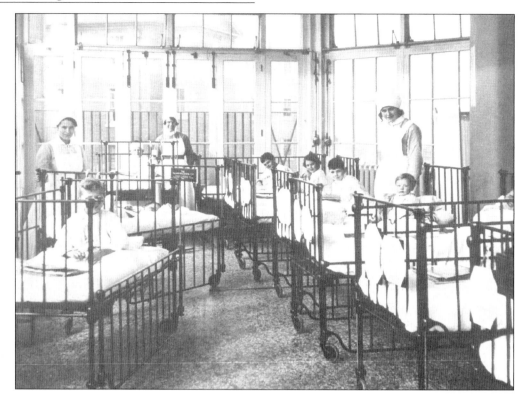

Ward in the children's hospital at the Leicester Royal Infirmary.

rubbed on the eczema, and it would clear it up within two days. Now that was fantastic.

Mrs C. Tebbutt

Angelica ointment

My mother and my grandma made their own ointment. Angelica was a plant that grew in the garden, and the thick stalks were cut and boiled, and then they used to get what they called leaf lard from the butcher's. Now I don't know what that is, but the liquid was strained and the lard was put into the rest of it, and then it was allowed to set, and it was poured into jars, and this was called angelica ointment. If you had a splinter, it would help you draw that splinter out if it was deep, instead of digging it out, it would draw it out. It was marvellous. And then my mum used to make her own cough mixture. You would get all different oils from the chemist. It had laudanum in it, so that was to help you sleep at night, obviously, and I forget what the other ingredient was, it's quite a strong thing and in most of the modern cough mixtures now. But my mum used to get these different things from the chemist and make it herself. That was done a lot in those days, your own remedies for almost everything.

Blanche Harrison

7 The Second World War

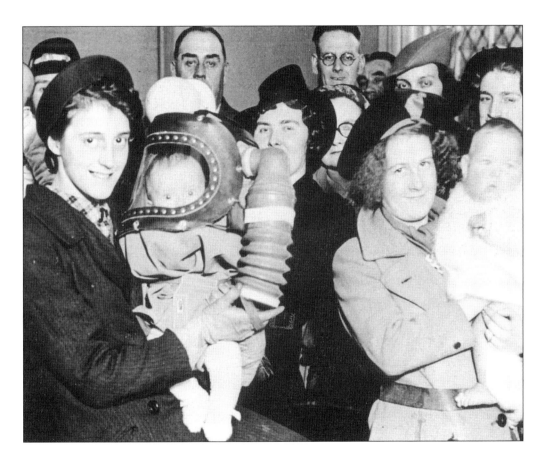

Baby's gas mask.

A quiet Sunday

I can remember the Sunday, because people after lunch on Sunday used to sit outside talking in the sunshine. But on that particular Sunday it was very quiet. And I particularly remember the next day because

I was down at the Boulevard collecting blackberries and I got my head stuck in the railings, and by the time I got back my father had gone. So I missed him going away. He was in the Territorial Army, the artillery.

Tony Hurst

Gas masks

There used to be little Mickey Mouse ones for small children, and for babies a type of thing with a hood over it, and you fastened it all up and pumped it with a handle. You were supposed to have tried them on and worn them for so many hours a day, or perhaps for ten minutes two or three times a day. It was supposed to be an offence not to have your gas mask with you.

Joan Fenwick

ARP messenger

They asked for volunteers for the ARP, and I volunteered on 3 August 1939. My brother volunteered on the same day, and I stayed in right to the end of the war, till you weren't required any more. I belonged to a cycling club. They were asking for messengers, so I volunteered as a messenger because I felt I could do more than any other way. You never knew what you were delivering, you were given whatever to go, and that was how it was. When they had air raids and things, they sent me to various schools to get information.

Freda Hales

Conscientious objector

I was a conscientious objector to the war. This arose out of my Christian commitment. It was very difficult to have views which were opposite to the vast majority of your countrymen, and to maintain those views in the face of intense pressure to go against them. Although I must say that in the main my working colleagues, who by this time were mainly women, and these women had got husbands and sons and brothers and lovers away, and some of them had been killed and injured, despite this fact there was quite a tolerance among them. I think they recognised that even though they disagreed with me, at least I was sincere in my beliefs.

Mr Lowe

Sandbagging

I can remember all the sandbagging, because us kids thought it was great and we used to help fill the bags. They used to have a special machine for filling the bags, and they used to tuck the end over and stack them up. It was done on the site outside the Technical College, covering it right to the top of the first floor windows, and they were about eight feet out at the base, and up to about two feet out at the top. I remember the old blackout every night. Yes, we had some special ones made with wood and black paper, and we used to fit them into the window at night time. And a lot of people had dark curtains. But as I say, ours were specially made.

Tony Hurst

Married on washday

My husband and I were engaged, and he was still on Reserve in the Guards, Cavalry, King's Dragoons. He went a couple of days before they were actually fetched, before we were going to get married – this was September – but of course all these plans went to pot, and he went to France straight away. He was over in France for three months until that Christmas. Then he came home a week before Christmas, on the Thursday, and we got married on the 18th of December, which was the Monday, at 10 o'clock in the morning. Washday, it was normally! We had a special licence of course, because he knew he was going to the Middle East, and he went off in the February, and I didn't see him again for four years.

Blanche Harrison

Sandbagging Charles Street Police Station.

More freedom

The evacuation from London was very well organized. There must have been several hundreds, mainly women and children. Not everybody wanted evacuees. These were mainly the elderly whose families had grown up, and did not want their homes invaded by strangers. It was completely different for me. Much more freedom in every respect. The house we lived in was a beautiful clean house. It did have an outside toilet, but this was for the one house only, not a shared toilet. It was much safer for us in Leicester after the initial Blitz of 1940 although there were still some scary times. We were quickly absorbed into the local population. All my brothers and sisters that came to Leicester with Mother and me have remained here.

Jim Baker

Billeting the children

They gave me the job of billeting children between the ages of six and ten, children who

89

had been evacuated to Leicester. A lot of the children I had to billet were from private homes, from private schools also, school uniform and all the rest, very, very nicely spoken kids, very polite kids. We went to Mundella School to do that, and then we had to go round the estate and advertise it, and then sit in a little office and wait for people to volunteer to have how many children, whatever they wanted, whether they were boys or girls, what ages, and I'd write it down and keep a log of it. And then on the day the children arrived an ARP officer and myself had to take them, then the families came and we'd sort them out. When you billeted children you kept a list and every so often you'd go and see if they were alright, check on the house, see if they were being treated well, and make sure the children had written

to their mothers. We used to say 'have you written to your mum?', and if they says 'no, I can't write very well', I said 'shall you and me sit down then and I'll help you?', so that's what we did. Then later on, when they were able to go back home again, we had quite a nice lot of letters from mums of the children, and I thought that was nice.

Freda Hales

Ducks in the bath

So eventually all the children were billeted out, but we still had to stay for two or three hours to see if there were any more queries. And this lady came back and said we'd billeted a boy at this address, and had we been? She said 'well, I think you should go',

Digging trenches in Town Hall Square.

ARP Messengers' Marching Band. The ARP were also responsible for billeting evacuee children.

so I went and found the address, found the boy, and he was in the bedroom crying his eyes out. When the door was opened there wasn't any stair treads on the stairs, there was no handrails, there was no doors on any of the rooms in the house, and we went up the stairs walking on the edges of the steps to get to him. It was a dreadful place, they'd got ducks in the bath, yes, ducks in the bath. So I picked his bag up and walked him back to the depot, but on the way back I was rubbing my face and I'd got fleas on me. I was covered in lice, and so was the boy. So we had to ring up to make arrangements for an empty van to come and fetch us and take us to the Cleansing Depot which was in Jarvis Street, and we were taken down there and deloused,

the boy and myself, all his luggage, all his clothes and everything, and then we had to come back and find somewhere else for him to go, and it was about ten o'clock at night before we found somewhere.

Freda Hales

Evacuees

I was living at Stoughton when the war started. One or two of the children came first, and then the Co-op gave them the loan of a cottage right at the side of the church. The windows looked out over the church garden, I don't know what they thought, the churchyard! I can see them now. The two girls

91

Bomb damage in Leicester in 1940. The worst raids were on 19-20 November 1940 during the Leicester 'Blitz'.

who had been here for a little while had got used to a very, very sleepy village with nothing going on, and then the rest of the family came and joined them. Oh dear, their faces! They thought they'd gone to the moon, I think. They'd never been anywhere like it, and the mother was absolutely devastated. I don't know how they ended up. I often think about those poor people coming from a very crowded area, the city, to a very sleepy village. It must have been awful for them.

Primrose Hall

More scary than the bombs

My overall impression of Leicester during the war years from a child's point of view was that it was an interesting city, safe, friendly. I missed the chocolate of course. We had quite a large garden, so there were a lot of things we grew ourselves. We also kept chickens, and it is amazing what you can get by bartering eggs, so generally we settled in well. We had quite a few air raid warnings, presumably when the planes came over on their way to and from Coventry, and whenever there was a raid we did spend part of the night in the air raid shelter, and one night we could hear bombs falling, that was quite frightening. It was not as frightening as the time when we were in Prague and I was told to stay in. As far as I can recall, the Germans were marching or having a demonstration. I do not know what was going on in the streets. That of course was far more scary than even the bombs were.

Tom Lawson

You got used to it

We used to get on the roof of the old Tech, and there was all wooden panelling up there. We used to sit up there and watch the raids, and one particular night, when Coventry got hit, we were actually on the roof and saw it all. In the distance there was a big glow in the sky, and you could actually see the explosions, or the aftermath of the explosions, and the flashes in the sky. We didn't think much about it at the time, we just watched it. We used to go up the tower of St Mary de Castro. There used to be a door behind the altar and it used to take you up through the belfry into the tower. We used to go up there quite a lot, we never got found out. The bomb on the Newarke Houses, oh yes, I remember that very well. In actual fact when they had shored it up and emptied it and closed it all down we made it into our gang headquarters.

The first air raid, we didn't realise what it was. But the next night I was waiting for it and I was terrified. I can remember my sister getting into my bed and holding me because I was shaking. And that was just in

Fire Force 9 HQ staff, National Fire Service, in Leicester.

anticipation of it. But after a while you got used to it and took no notice, didn't even bother. You never used the air raid shelters. My first bit of shrapnel, I got that from the Newarkes, digging in the craters just outside. A big thing at school, it were, swapping bits and bobs, bullets, bits of shells, cartridge cases, anything you could lay your hands on.

Tony Hurst

Working on the trams

I was in the shoe trade at the start of the war. I was twenty-two and I stayed put for the time being because my husband went overseas and he wanted to know I was still in Leicester. I'd worked in the shoe trade since leaving school. The boss had it deferred twice, but the third time I had to go, it was 1941 and I had a choice: Land Army, the Services, munitions or transport. My friends were mostly in munitions, but I'd been in a factory and I didn't want that again. So I chose transport, and for me it turned out to be the trams.

There were strict rules. Even in wartime you were fetched into the office if you were reported for anything. You could be reported for leaving a runner. You know, for turning a blind eye, as it were, because there were no cars, you see. People weren't allowed to use petrol, and so everyone, munitions workers, the lot, all depended on the transport, and that was made known to you, oh yes. You'd get reported if you had a smoke on the platform of your tram, you were in the wrong. I mean, you weren't supposed to do it really, but they were very strict rules then, when I went out on it, which was fair enough. It kept things going much more smoothly, shall I say.

Blanche Harrison

Always late

When I was working, I started here in Oadby, but they soon transferred me, and I ended up working right across the other side of Leicester, up Abbey Lane. Quite a few of us used to go. During the war we used to catch the first bus out of Oadby at five to seven. There wasn't one before. We had to be up Abbey Lane for half past seven, but we were always late, all of us, because there was no other way. We used to jump off the bus at the Midland Station, jump on the tram to the Clock Tower, jump off that one more or less while it was still going, run across the road and get on the next one for Abbey Lane. This was when I worked for Taylor Hobson's.

Primrose Hall

English Glass Company

Both parents worked full-time at the English Glass Company, trying to make the glass-making company into a positive balance. It originally employed two to three people, some of them part-time. This was in the 30s, but during the war it became a thriving manufacturing concern with over sixty employees, producing glass products which were, a lot of them, vital to the war effort, as well as glass hat pins, buttons, costume jewellery, and other technical products for the telephone, and the military. The reason that the company were able to do so many consumer products was that all imports had stopped coming into the country, and there was a society called the Limbless Society, a disabled society, which employed people who were damaged from the First and Second World War, and they had several factories where they made up products for resale. Their outlets were Woolworth's and a few other large companies. If one was making products for the Limbless Society and

Gimson's Ambulance Brigade in 1940.

employed disabled people, then one got special permission for extra fuel and extra raw materials which were in short supply, to produce special products.

Tom Lawson

Potato picking

Oh, the war to me when it first started was nothing. We heard about it, people spoke about it, but nothing happened. Then, when the first air raid came, we realised we'd got a war on us hands and things began to change. Everybody started working for the war effort, and I mean everybody, everybody did a little bit. Even up to the age of thirteen I can

remember doing things to help the war effort. We used to have a van outside for the paper. We used to have a bag outside for the tins, and you could only put rubbish in the dustbin that you couldn't save. In fact, they did more recycling during the war than they do now and, mind, the vehicles were different then, you can't cater for it now with the type of vehicles we've got, I mean, the old vehicles used to have big hooks on the back, and as they went by they'd have maybe twenty or thirty bags hanging on the back for paper and tins.

When we were at St Martin's school, when the potato season was in we used to go potato picking, and I think we used to get about five bob a week. I know it wasn't a lot, but we were allowed to bring as many potatoes as we wanted home. And I can remember that every boy that came in used to have to give the Headmaster two potatoes every day. Of course, at the end of a week he'd got enough potatoes to last him a year. But I used to like that, playing on the farms at dinner time. Mind it was all horses and carts then. The old wagons, big shires, we used to look forward to that. The City Council provided a bus and there used to be twenty-five or thirty pupils from our school (there were only ninety at the school) and then the following week another twenty or thirty would go and that is how it worked.

Tony Hurst

The hole in the wall

The Gas Office ran from Market Street round into Pocklington's Walk, and during the war there used to be a permanently lit gas jet coming from a hole in the wall. You can see where they bricked it up now. You couldn't get matches, and all the men used to queue up to light a fag at this gas jet.

Vernon Spong

A rough loaf

Prior to the Second World War breaking out there was all the talk of rationing, and coupons and everything, and as my father was in the dairying the Milk Marketing Board issued all the coupons about how much butter, margarine, lard and eggs everyone got, as they were all rationed, and he had to keep count for all the customers so they got their fair share. We were in the baking, and that was also rationed as far as bread was concerned. Our drivers, our roundsmen, were all called up for National Service, and so

therefore my husband and his brother had to manage to do all the baking and the deliveries themselves, and then they had to come back at night and make the dough up, wait till it rose, then bake the bread, take it out of the ovens and run them off on the round themselves, and that was a very, very trying time. We wives, we helped to do what we could.

During the war a lot of the refined flour that we used to get was stopped altogether, it was what they called Canadian flour, which was the strong flour. And it was more of a rough loaf. All of the beautiful white bread had to go, and they had to make do with what you would really term as seconds in the flour. So therefore it was more of a roughish bread.

Mrs C. Tebbutt

Anything to feed you

We had an allotment on Gwendolen Road, near the City General Hospital, and we used to fill it full of food, best we could, because with seven of us we got through some food and it was difficult. We'd try to make jam, because we got all our fruit together, so we either bottled it in Kilner jars, or made jam, or bottled the fruit as it was. It didn't really matter, as long as we got some food. You see, if you got jam and an egg you could make up sponge pudding or something, or spotted dick. The time was spent really queuing for your ration. You perhaps spent an hour and a half, two hours, queuing, and when you came home perhaps all you'd got was two rashers of bacon or half a pound of sausages, between seven of you. It was toad in the hole, perhaps, because if you had any sausages you'd cut them down length-wise in half and make a big Yorkshire pudding, and one half you'd put the sausages in, and in the other half you could perhaps put something else in, apple rings, something like that, anything to feed you. Rabbits used to go a long way because if you had a big fat nice rabbit that would be four days dinner, wouldn't it. One day roasted, the next day stewed, the next day extra vegetables in with the gravy, and things like this.

Freda Hales

Eggs and everything

We dug part of the garden up to set vegetables. We had our own poultry, so therefore we'd got eggs and everything, and if there was a shortage of meat we'd got the chicken that we could kill and have at the weekends. Quite a lot of people dug their lawns up to grow vegetables: potatoes, carrots, onions, cabbages and all sorts of things. We didn't keep meat in as such. I mean we had thralls in the pantries, and they were made either of brick or marble, we used to have a marble slab in our pantry, and kept our meat cool like that. And then we had covers for the meat, but there were not the fridges as there are today.

Mrs C. Tebbutt

How do you do for food?

We'd perhaps go off on our bikes and go to a Youth Hostel for the weekend, because they were open all the time, and people would say 'you live in the city, how do you do for food?' And I said 'ever so poorly', and they said 'oh well, we've got bees, we'll give you two pound jars, so when you went cycling you always took two pound jam jars with you, you see. Well, that was a godsend, because you could make cake with it, or you could put it in your drinks. Sugar was as short as the devil, such a small allowance that anything like that was a godsend.

We went to the Wymeswold Youth Hostel, and the warden's wife took ill so I said, 'go on, I'll help you out'. Later they brought me home in a lorry, and they said 'you better take this box with you, and it was this big wooden box, an army surplus box, and somebody had killed a pig, so they gave me a pork joint. And somebody had made some brawn with some of the pork, and they gave me a big basin full of brawn, all pressed, lovely fresh, you see, and then they said to me 'what are you short of most', and I said 'well, eggs, things that make a meal', and so they said 'would two dozen eggs be nice?', and I said 'wouldn't it!' And that was absolutely fantastic. Inside the box we found a tin of jam, and then there were four lovely loaves, home baked loaves the bakery had put in for me because I'd helped them out. And of course, if the blackberries were in season, or if there were apples, you'd see on the fence 'Apples fallen, penny a pound' or something, and you'd fill your saddlebag with apples or blackberries, anything that would make a meal in some form.

Freda Hales

Yankee army!

The Americans woke us up, I think! Oadby was still only a village back then. A lot of them were country boys themselves. They had tents on the Racecourse and certainly at Shady Lane, but they used what is now the old swimming pool. They boarded the floor over, you know, and I think that was their mess hall. And we used to have a village hall, and they used to go there. And of course we'd got a cinema, and they used to go in the cinema. We used to speak to them, and I remember one used to give all the children, the little boys and girls, a ride round the village in his jeep. I've got a lovely poem about them:

Troops of the US 82nd Airborne Division stationed in Leicester before the D-Day landings in 1944.

Dear old England's not the same,
We dreaded invasion when it came,
But now it's not the beastly Hun,
The Goddamned Yankee Army's come.
We see them in the train and bus,
There isn't room for all of us,
We walk to let them have our seat,
And then get run over by their jeep!

Primrose Hall

Good to the children

I can remember the Americans. There used to be a hot dog stall in the Humberstone Gate. I can remember they were threepence apiece, and the Americans used to wait there to catch the bus going home at night. And of course they were buying hot dogs, and we used to go up to them 'Could you buy us a hot dog mister?' and nine times out of ten you got one. Very good, they were. They used to have a store down the old cricket ground, in the pavilion. We used to lark down there as kids and we went in it once. I don't know if it was open or whether it had been broke open, but we found all the rations, the iron rations the Americans used to have. I can remember one big box and a cup of little cigarettes in this little packet, twenty-four hour packs, and I took quite a few home, which in actual fact came in handy to eat. The word got round that it was open and everybody started going until the Americans twigged it and then boarded it all up.

The white Americans tended to stick round the Clock Tower area. But if you went down say Humberstone Road and you got into one or two of the outlying pubs say on Brunswick Street, there used to be one on the corner there. The coloured Americans used to get in that one, and that is it what it was like round Leicester on the peripheral – coloured Americans.

Tony Hurst

Chocolate and pineapple

The Americans thought we were starving, and they used to stand at the bus stop and hand something to everybody who got off the bus, and I remember my sister running home, and when she got home she'd got an egg in her hand, and she daren't squeeze it, you see. Well, they'd given her an egg, and they used to give us chocolate and tins of pineapple. We'd hadn't seen tins of pineapple since before the war, you see.

Primrose Hall

Good times

We had some good times. We went out when we could. We went to the theatre sometimes, and the cinema - the old Opera House. We would go and queue there for the 'pits', and that was a shilling. And in the cinema, if the alarm went, 'Moaning Minnie' we used to call it, we could either stay put 'cos they

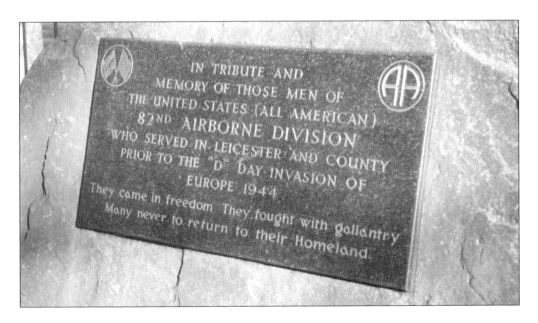

Memorial to men of the US 82nd Airborne on Victoria Park, Leicester.

Preparations for the D-Day invasion in 1944 – a group of Royal Engineers.

would stop the show, but in the cinema they had an organist, and he would play music. We used to sit a little while, then we'd get fed up and walk home. No lights, no street lights, you know. The American soldiers used to go in pubs in the centre. They were always the best-off regarding money, oh yes.

Blanche Harrison

D-Day

I remembered D-Day as we were in the Regal Cinema and a flash came up on the screen telling us that D-Day had started. It wasn't the actual day, but I can remember it going up on the screen, and I can remember everybody sitting or standing on their seats and shouting 'fantastic!' I don't think we took any interest in the picture after that. Everybody had been waiting for it to happen, and everybody was saying 'it's going to be today, it's going to be today', and when it

happened everybody was elated. Everybody expected it, and they expected it every day, but when it came, magic! I'd seen the build up. A lot of convoys used to come through Leicester, and sometimes you would get held up for half an hour waiting for the convoys to go through. You could tell it was coming.

Tony Hurst

Italian prisoners of war

We had Italian prisoners of war working on the railways, and they used to do the work we were doing. They were stationed on the Aylestone Road. They used to come in a Timson's removal truck. When I first saw them, knowing they were enemies, I was terrified when one came near me. When I got to know them they were quite pleasant. They didn't seem to mind that they were prisoners, in fact some of their food was a lot better than what we were bringing for lunch. If we started to sing, they'd join in, and if they saw you struggling with a very heavy bag, they'd be there to help you.

Beryl Richardson

Really lovely singing

Of course, we had the German prisoners here, in Shady Lane. They worked on the farms. The only ones I knew were the ones we had at Stoughton. I don't know how many they had, but they got on alright with them. A lot of them were very young, I mean some of them weren't much older than us fifteen year old children, you know. I remember those who worked in Oadby Lodge, because the people there were friends of ours, and they used to spend a lot of their time cutting out, making marvellous tin toys out of a sardine tin or a treacle tin, and they made wooden toys. And I remember when they first came and they were camped on Shady Lane, because the Americans built the billets on Shady Lane, then they went, and they started bringing the German prisoners over. It was a regular Sunday evening walk from Oadby to Shady Lane. I don't know what I expected to see, you couldn't see much anyway, but I can always remember their singing. They were obviously locked in on Sundays, you see, when they weren't working on the farm, but oh, their singing, it was really lovely.

Primrose Hall

VE Day

What a night! There were thousands down town. Town Hall Square was packed solid all the way down to the Clock Tower, you couldn't walk along the road. In actual fact it was the first time I'd had a drop of beer, that night. Some soldier gave me a drink out of his bottle and he'd got a pack full of them. And I can remember all the lights in the Square, yes, I can remember them all coming on, and it was magic to walk around to see all the shops with lights on after living in the dark for all them years. Our street party was in Pentonville – we used to call them puddings back then, no through traffic – and I can remember there were two rows of tables. Don't ask me where all the linen came from, and don't ask me where all the grub came from, but we didn't half have a lot to eat. I think the shops supplied all the pop, and I know it went on for two or three hours. Then at night time they all started dancing again. And VJ Day was another celebration, but it was nothing like VE Day.

Tony Hurst

Quand Madelon vient nous servir à boire...
(French march)

A postcard from France.

VE Day street party in Leicester.

Flying the regimental flag

Eventually I became the senior warrant officer in the camp. Even then, being only in my mid-twenties, you'll realise the terrible losses that we'd undertaken. There were twenty-three or twenty-four of us in this camp, and I had a whisper from some Siamese people that the Japanese were going to surrender, because they were in a hell of a mess. And then we heard that these two bombs had dropped. We didn't know they were atom bombs, just huge bombs, and the Japanese then had surrendered. I had a thought that, when we did take over the camp, I wanted straight away to mark it as our camp, but I realised that a Union Jack would be too complicated to make, so I thought we'd try and make a Regimental flag. We had a lad with us named Lance-Corporal Carter, he was a good tailor, and for obvious reasons was nicknamed Tack. So we stole the underskirt of a Korean prostitute, who were named comfort women and who were stationed about five or six kilometres from our camp in a caravan that the Japanese soldiers used to visit. We also stole a Japanese officer's pith helmet, tropical helmet. Inside it was a red lining which we wanted. The Korean prostitute's underskirt was black. We also got a clean white loincloth that we all wore, because by then we'd got no clothes. And Tack Carter made this Regimental flag, with our Regimental colours of red, pearl grey and black, and this was the nearest we could get, of course, and in the centre of it we put the figures XVII. We were the 17th Regiment of Foot, as we were formed in 1688. And as soon as the Japanese commandant told me that they'd finished, and that we were now free, we hoisted this flag on the tallest bamboo pole that we could find, and flew it over the camp. Before I left the camp, I had the flag taken down, and I had all the lads sign it with a bit of indelible pencil or whatever we could find.

Harry Oates

VJ Day

We had the VJ bonfire on the corner at the top of the street. Nearly every street had one, they were clearing all the old houses out and building new stuff, getting the [Eyres] Monsall ready for building. The object was to start it the day before, start somebody else's. Ingenious ways we used to do it. You'd get some petrol from somewhere and throw a jam jar so it would break, and we used to stand on the corner – and we used to make really good

bows and arrows and we'd set fire to it.

Anonymous male contributor (1)

Fainting with the shock

He came home, I knew that he was on his way but of course you never knew when, and it was getting dark and this knock came at the door. I think it was about nine and ten in the evening, and Bob had travelled a long, long while, and he'd got his gear on, and looked dirty and that, and he just stood at the front door. I knew he was on his way, but you know, no way did I know he was going to show up at the door. I went to the door, and he stood there. I mean, this is after four years! What did I do? Only fainted, didn't I? My Grandma, she told me off, scandalous. 'The very idea of fainting!' It was just the shock, you see, I couldn't believe my eyes! Bob was one of the lucky ones. He got his job back. He had a job at the Gas Works, but his job was guaranteed and he was allowed so much money, that was to secure him for when he came back, you see. So yes, he was fine.

Blanche Harrison

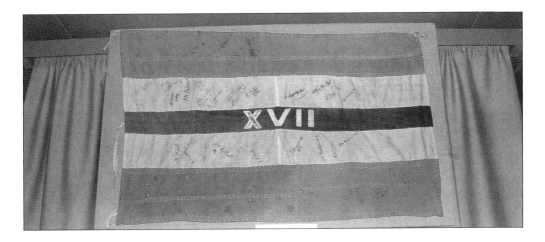

The Leicestershire Regiment flag made by Prisoners of War in Burma, on display in New Walk Museum, Leicester.

8 Shopping

The Victorian Fish Market in Leicester – but fish was also sold by horse and cart well into the twentieth century.

Lovely fresh fish

There was Mr Hall the fishmonger. He used to come round twice a week on Wednesdays and Fridays during the morning. And he'd got a piebald pony, I well remember that, with an open dray, and he'd just got a cover over the top of the fish, and it was all open to the elements. But none of us died with diseases! That was beautiful fish, really fresh lovely fish.

Mrs C. Tebbutt

Kirby & West milk cart in the 1930s.

The milk round

I was born in Dunster Street, and my mother and father had a dairy there. We had two milk rounds, one was all round the West End, the other down the North. Dad had a field on Sykefield Avenue that is now Barclay Street, the top end of Barclay Street, and he bred his own horses there. He used to fetch the milk, mostly from a farm, Braunstone Spinneys, at the back of the Braunstone Spinneys, that is the Braunstone Crossroads now, and he used to go there round about half past five to six o'clock in the morning. We made our own butter, separated the cream, and we used to open up, to start to sell milk at the dairy, from about seven o'clock in the morning till half past eleven at night. That was every day of the week bar Sunday, and we used to close at half past two on Sunday. And there'd still be people coming shouting 'Mr Lord, I want some milk', and the same at twelve o'clock at night! When Dad used to be on the round, he used to shout to the customers before he got there 'The Lord is with you!' Hundreds of pounds of butter I've made up with the butter pats on the marble slab.

Mrs C. Tebbutt

Sixpenny-worth of herrings

You know what Reg used to like to do Saturday nights, 'cos his dad was very fond of herrings, you know, when they're smoked, and his mother used to have to smoke them. So she used to send him for sixpenny-worth of herrings on a Saturday night. He used to love it 'cos he went on top of the tram, open tram, all the way to Leicester from Aylestone Park to the fish shop, and come back with his herrings for his mother on Saturday night.

Vernon Spong

Shrimps in baskets

Shrimps! Oh, that's an old thing. They used to take the baskets into pubs, and there were shrimps in the baskets. The oyster shop was up towards the Old Cross, of course the Old Cross isn't there any more. The Old Cross was on the junction of Charles Street and Belgrave Gate at one time. Of course, when they widened Charles Street, well of course that went.

Mr Walton

Fetching the meat

My father always used to go to a certain butcher. His name was Smith, on Narborough Road. I used to go Friday nights and then Saturday afternoons to deliver the meat. He did ask me then if I'd go early in the mornings in the week. So – I was thirteen – I said yes. It meant money to my mother, obviously. I should be down at the meat shop on Narborough Road at seven o'clock, then his assistant and I would go and collect a push-cart, and take this along right into the town to where the Telecom buildings were, opposite the Police Station, because that was the ice cold storage buildings. We'd go there and we would give us order in. We should get a side of beef and two or three lambs, and liver and kidneys and that kind of thing, and then we'd push the darned thing back right to the shop, and get there about half past eight. I did that three or four mornings a week.

William Lenton

The tripe man

The tripe man, he used to come round every Friday evening with his van, an open back van, and a huge bath full of tripe with all the liquor in it, and people used to go to him, it would be about half past seven every Friday evening, and take their jugs or basins, and have, well they sold it in pints then, because they sold it in measures. That was very cheap in those days, and that was another nutritious meal. You had the liquor with it, if you'd got a pound of tripe or two pounds of tripe, with the weed as well, the dark tripe was what they called the weed, and you would add a pint of milk and onions, and simmer it for about an hour. Some people liked it thickened and served with creamed potatoes, but I always liked bread and butter with mine, and that was another lovely meal.

Mrs C. Tebbutt

Fetching the tripe

Mrs Biddles had a tripe shop in Redcross Street. It was the only place on the right-hand side of Redcross Street, and she used to prepare and cook the tripe, cow heels, all that sort of stuff. She had a copper at the back of the place, two big coppers, which she used to boil the stuff in, and I used to go down every Saturday morning for my mother to fetch tripe. It was beautiful, beautiful! There was two places in Leicester, there was Mrs Biddles on Redcross Street, and her brother had a place on Humberstone Road, just beyond Curzon Street, on the left-hand side. The people used to queue for it when you'd go on Saturday morning. Money was scarce in them days, and people had to buy the cheapest stuff possible to live on, and tripe was one of the best. We used to boil the tripe. We had that for Saturday's dinner, and the liquor, we used to go down to the Argentine butcher's shop and purchase some shin of beef. Mother used to cut it up and put it into the liquor and put it on the old fashioned range, and she'd leave it there to stew for the whole of the rest of Saturday afternoon and all Saturday night,

One of the last cattle and sheep markets in Leicester in November 1988.

and on Sunday morning she used to strain it, and she used to say to me 'Are you going to have some, Cecil, for your breakfast?'. And believe me, honestly, it used to stick round your jaws, it was that good, it was beautiful. All the meat had gone down to practically nothing, just a tiny bit of meat.

Cecil Harris

Ice cream

I remember the first ice cream man on Saffron Lane. He had a wagon and it had a roof on it, like a mobile carousel. Altobell, his name was. This was late '40s, because it was motorised, and these poles used to go on the running board to hold this big roof on. A proper Italian with black hair and a moustache, I can see him now.

Anonymous male contributor (1)

Getting the coal

The coalman used to come round with the open drays, and the sacks of coal, and my Mother and Father used to have a ton at a time, they're called Derby Brights, and it would be stacked up right to the very top of the coalhouse, and that was wonderful coal. Some people would have just one bag, and when they sold coke in those days it was ninepence a sack of coke, and today I've no idea how much they would pay for it. And some people used to fetch it themselves, in a wheelbarrow or anything, for half the price from the coal wharves at the West Bridge.

Mrs C. Tebbutt

Leicester Market in the early twentieth century.

Going to the Gas Works

We used to have to go and get coke for the fires. If it got cold you used to have to go and get the bags and go down to the Gas Works, take the old pram. You used to have to go down and queue for it, literally queue all the way up the road, and you would only get a limited amount. You couldn't have too much, because obviously they weren't making it, because coal wasn't coming in after the war, and you could only have, say, a quarter. I can remember taking my brother's big pram, you know, a big coachwork-built pram, and filling it full of coke. And then I'd clean it out and he'd be in it. You had to get up quite early in the morning and queue, because otherwise you wouldn't get any, it would be all gone. I can remember that winter of 1947, the snow being so deep that you had to walk in a tyre track where the milk float had been, because it was like a channel.

Jackie Harvey

The Market Place

The Market Place used to be the place in those days. There used to be Blackburn's the lino people, who used to shout and auction the lino off. Then there was the mushy peas man. My husband used to love it, his mother said if she ever lost him she knew where to find him, 'cos he used to have sausages, and that was my husband's favourite. And the mushy peas, yes, all on the coke burners, weren't they? Then they'd have the ice cream tent with a big coke burner going in the middle and you'd sit and eat ice cream. Oh, it was a great life in those days! The old fish market, you'd go in there, you'd get your fish or whatever you wanted, and round the back of it was all animals – cats and rabbits. And then there was the Jetty wine shop, and the Oriental

The Market in the 1990s.

Café, Wynn's, at the top. We used to go there dancing. It later became a Woolworth's. You had everything there, you'd get a lipstick, you'd get a drawing pad, you'd get anything. In my days it was just paper, writing paper, lipsticks, all fancy stuff.

Anonymous female contributor (1)

Open till ten

Leicester Market used to be open until 10 p.m. on Saturdays. If they didn't stay open they wouldn't get any custom. I know that because my uncle and me dad used to work on Leicester Market Place and they'd got their own stall there, and it used to be midnight past before they used to get home.

Jackie Harvey

A lift up the ladder

Dad had bought this little old shop down in Brook Street, off Wharf Street. Very run down dilapidated place, and of course it was quite a lift up the ladder because Dad had had various jobs over the years, and this was something on his own. We used to be open at about half past six in the morning till about eight o'clock at night, and it used to be up until nine o'clock at night or thereabouts on a Friday, seven o'clock on a Saturday and all day on a Sunday. You were in and out the shop all the time, and if you took in those very early days forty or fifty pounds a week, you were doing very well indeed. And then, when it got to holiday times, when it got to Easter, Whit, Christmas or the week's holiday they used to have in August, people didn't get paid, so they invariably couldn't pay you, and we used to have to say 'Don't worry about that money. We'll put that on the back of the book. Pay it off so much a week'. Well, by the time they'd paid it off at about two bob a week, there was another holiday upon them, so consequently there was this amount of money with quite a lot of customers owing it in the back of the book, and I'm sure we had lots and lots of money owed to us.

Ernie White

No closing times

The opening hours were practically all day, really. We had no closing times in those days. It was supposed to be fishing tackle only, almost opposite St Mark's church, and it was the only fishing tackle shop to sell fishing tackle alone. You see, there was Clark's gunsmith's, Keen's, they had a little bit of fishing tackle, usually sea fishing. Well, ours was the canals and that. We did a very good

trade. We had more trade on a Sunday because we had close seasons, I can't remember the dates now. And then the best part of the year we used to rely on the boat people, canal people, the boaters. They used to stay in the basin, the bottom of [St Mark's] church, where the canal came to an end, and they used to park there, you see, and they used to come and buy their kit in the winter.

Mrs Walton

Rows of shops

Little streets, many, many little streets with many little corner shops, and sometimes whole rows, especially along Wharf Street, some of which opened on a Sunday. In Taylor Street there was Mancini's that sold ice cream and sweets, very, very nice ice cream. There was Smith's the grocer's at the corner of Denmark Street and Taylor Street. Worthington's at the corner of Brunswick

Bill White's shop in Brook Street.

Shops on Belgrave Gate in the 1930s.

Street, and opposite the school on the other side of Taylor Street was Alma Cottages with Stanion the undertaker, and they dropped a bomb on part of his building on 19 November 1940. There wasn't a pane of glass touched in the school, but a bomb fell on part of his works. Next to him was Greasley's the baker, and Marvin the Post Office. And if you went further down, right to the end of Brunswick Street, next to the factory was Henfrey's boot and shoe shop, a very friendly little place. Mr Henfrey mended all our boots and shoes. He was old fashioned, you know, hammering the nails in.

Margaret Zientek

A good shopping area

It was a good shopping area, Wharf Street was, very good. A lot of shops down Wharf Street were there for years. Some big shops, really. On the corner of Erskine Street there used to be like a fashion salon, Jacob's, sold furs and things like that, and further down Wharf Street there was Marvin's, that was quite a big store, it was. You sort of got to know your own local shops, but you see, the town was so near as well. I mean, you did your shopping in the Market sometimes, although the shops were good on Wharf Street. And fish and chip shops, there was ample of them.

Shops on Hinckley Road in the 1980s.

There were shops everywhere, you'd got no need to move out of Wharf Street, you could get everything you wanted.

Iris Smith

Blue bags for the sugar

At the corner of Dunster Street there used to be Worthington's and they used to packet all their own tea, and all their own sugar. It used to come in big sacks, and then the assistants would weigh all the sugar into pounds, they used to be blue packs, the bags, blue bags that they used to have for the sugar. The cheese and butter, that was all weighed up at the corner shop. It was a really busy little area, all round in Dunster Street. Where all the shops are now at the top of Bolton Road, it was just open ground, and they'd got advertising boards all along there. That was all open ground straight down to the brook where we all used to go and play, jumping over the water and falling in.

Mrs C. Tebbutt

Hundreds of birds

Then there was Berry's, the fish people. As a lad I always used to stand amazed at the poultry they used to have hanging up on hooks outside, and at night-time they used to drop a sheet over it to protect it. But I should think if there was one bird of some description, I bet there must have been nearly a hundred. As a lad, I can always remember it.

Cecil Harris

112

Bacon hocks, soup & faggots

We used to cook bacon hocks, soak them overnight, then the next day we would boil them up in the old copper in the kitchen and sell them hot at threepence or fourpence each. People used to come and order these things! And then the next day the liquor that they'd been cooked in used to set solid, all this jelly, so we'd take the top scum off, and then we used vegetables, things like carrots and parsnips and things like that, and grate them up into the soup, boil it up again, and we'd sell that as hot soup on Friday at twopence a pint, and that really used to go like wildfire! I can see them coming in now with a jug of ale in one hand and another jug, or even things that are unmentionable, for a couple of pints of soup! We used to cook faggots, we used to sell faggots at two for three halfpence or a penny each. We also used to do mushy peas, hot pig's belly, black pudding, all this sort of thing we sold on a Friday. On Saturdays we used to make our own ice cream. We used to make it with sterilised milk, ice cream powder, pour it into a drum similar to a butter paddle in the middle, and churn away. Our old dad used to have us turning that runny stuff till it was absolutely full, because the more you turned it, obviously the more it made.

Ernie White

Don't forget the number

I was thinking about the Co-op. I loved that place. I suddenly remembered my auntie's Co-op number. They used to drill it into you, 'Don't forget the number', get your divi.

Jackie Harvey

The Co-op fish department

If the man on the Co-op fish department lorry used to go on holiday, or when he was ill, they called on me to go and do his work because I knew the round, you see. I used to report down the traffic department at five o'clock in the morning, get this van out – it was a flat-backed lorry – and I used to pick up the manager, Jack Ford, in Bakewell Street in Highfields, and we'd drive to the railway station and pick up fish from there, and we'd drive to the other station, Central, and pick up fish from there in fish boxes, then we'd drive to the wholesale fish market, which was in Vestry Street at that time.

We used to drive slowly through the market. On either side of the Vestry Street fish market were fishmongers with boxes of

Shopping at the Co-op – an advertisement from 1915.

fish of all sorts, and the manager would be on foot in front of me, ordering the various fish, you see, as I drove by very slowly, at a walking pace, while the staff, the fish men, would load the lorry until it was complete. Then we used to drive round to the fish and fruit depot in Bond Street, and by the time we got there it was round about six o'clock, or just gone six. There used to be two cutters there, Wal Irons and Harry Goodwin, and they used to cut the fish up. They used to cut up the various orders for the various branches, you see, because at that time there was about over fifty-odd branches of the Co-op, and some of the grocery departments sold fish as well. They had five fish departments, five fish shops, attached to the stores. So I used to go round and deliver them. I used to work then from five in the morning until half past one, have the afternoons off, and on Wednesday

The shop referred to in this extract was Kempin's tobacconist's, shown here in 2002.

afternoon and Friday afternoon I used to go round the shops and pick up the empty crates and boxes, and pick up the empties for the greengrocery department as well.

Anonymous male contribuutor (2)

The smell of Bruno Tobacco

I think I learned from the customers, you know, because they'd come in for an ounce of Bruno and they'd say, 'I don't want it in a packet, I want it out of the tin' 'cos we sold it loose as well as packed. But a certain amount of different tobaccos you sold loose, and they'd tell you which they wanted. It was a lovely smell to open a freshly opened tin of Bruno, eleven pence an ounce. I don't know what it is now! And then, of course, there was the snuff. Well, of course, I'd no idea about snuff and it was in, I should think they were two-pound tins. And it was loose, this particular snuff, this 'SP' that we used to sell. We sold various snuffs but a lot of it was packed. But then we sold quite a lot that wasn't packed. We used to have a policeman come in. Well, he was my first customer and he asked for these quarters of snuff because he took them for the police at the police station, and he always demanded to have it weighed up while he was there. So, of course, he said 'quarters of snuff', you see, so of course I went on measuring quarter of pounds of snuff and he stopped me on the third pack, and I remember it was the third quarter, and he said 'I think you're wrong'. So my boss came in at that particular time, and she said 'What are you doing?' So I said, 'I'm weighing the snuff up for Mr Shepherd, the policeman'. So she said, 'No, not quarter of pounds, quarter of ounces'. He let me do the third, he was enjoying it, wasn't he! Pulled my leg for many years.

We dressed the window every Thursday as well as the pipes and things that were in the display. There was a brass bowl with loose

Chamberlain's cycle shop on Clarendon Park Road, decorated for a shop window competition in 1937.

tobacco put in it to display in the shop, and we used to display the shag and things like that in it, you see. They were all fetched out on Thursday night and I had to sit after we'd shut the shop and polish every pipe, and they were always done with shoe polish, brown shoe polish. Every pipe that had been in the window. So we never had any faded pipes! And the lighters were polished.

Anonymous female contributor (2)

Joseph Johnson's

Joseph Johnson's was a family shop. It was a beautiful shop. When the wealthy people had their motor cars driven by a chauffeur, the lady of the house would arrive at Joseph Johnson's, and if it was raining there was a doorman there with a huge umbrella. He'd go to the car doors – you're not allowed to get a drop of rain on her - shelter her under this umbrella to the entrance of the shop. And if

you went up into the restaurant (there was a nice restaurant) there was a supervisor there to lead you round the restaurant and show you to a table. You were really looked after in shops in those days. There were shop walkers, they were usually men in frock coats, to lead you to a chair. 'Madam wants serving?' Madam was seated, the assistant came. It was different altogether. Mind you, you couldn't go and look around the shops and handle goods like you can now. You were shown a certain selection, and sometimes the assistant would try one on herself and walk round so you could see what it looked like.

Mona Lewis

Simpkin & James

They used to bottle there too. Wine used to come in to us in casks, and we had to bottle. When wine came in, one had to look at its clarity, and if the clarity was such that it needed

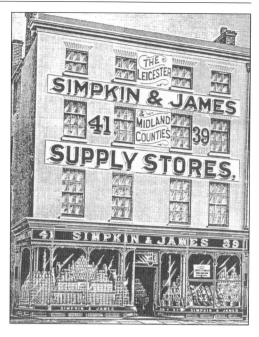

Late nineteenth century advertisement for Simpkin & James.

Market Street in the evening, and you could hear perhaps a piano going in the top storey, and the girls would be hanging out seeing the world go by. I think it must have been a bit of a horrific life I suppose they had, no family life, probably. Indifferent kinds of meals and accommodation.

Mona Lewis

Lewis'

Lewis' was built in 1934/35, 'cos I was off school then with a septic ankle and my dad was off work with a broken arm, and we used to hobble down to Lewis' site and watch this huge crane, which was the first one in Leicester, swinging all the girders into position. And at the back, between Lewis' and Marks & Spencer's where that road is, were huge boilers.

Vernon Spong

treatment in the form of filings to clarify it, then one had to sort of try and associate the amount of wine filings that needed to be added to clarify the actual wine. Christmas was undoubtedly the busiest time of the year in the wine and spirit trade. I seem to think that one's turnover would be about a third of the annual turnover, at least, you would do in the month, six weeks, prior to Christmas. You'd begin to get a build-up from the beginning of November right through to Christmas Eve, and we always used to look upon Christmas Eve as being the climax, particularly on the shop side, the cash side of it. We used to have tremendous queues of people for wine.

John Clarke

Living over the shop

The shop girls lived on the top storey of Herrington's. I remember walking down

Lewis's store in Humberstone Gate. The store has now been demolished, but the landmark tower has been retained as part of a new shopping centre.

9 Coming to Leicester

Leicester's relative prosperity in the 1930s attracted many people in search of work.

Moving from the country

I always remember my grandma taking me, 'cos my mum couldn't leave 'cos she'd got the family you'd see. My grandma brought me to Leicester and the first thing she did was take me into a hat shop and buy me a new hat and white gloves. And then I was taken up to London Road to the shop where I was going to work and where I was going to live, 'cos I couldn't travel every day backwards and forwards, well there were no buses anyway. And there I was left. It was a long day when my grandma had gone and left me. I was in the shop trying to adapt myself to everything. And I always remember, my aunt lived not far away in the Highfields area – my mum's sister – and my boss said to me, 'would you like to go and see your aunt?' I said, 'Ooh yes please!' I thought, well if I get there, shall I come back? But I did, I came back.

Anonymous female contributor (2)

Plenty of work in Leicester

I left Wales in 1923. My brother couldn't get a job and I was working in a shop at three shillings (15p) a week. My aunties lived here, and they came to live in Leicester in 1913 because of the depression – there was no work in Wales then. One of my aunties made a friend of a Leicester girl, and she came to Leicester for a holiday and she liked Leicester so much she got a job. There was plenty of work in Leicester at the time. So they came to Leicester.

In 1923 we had no work, I was only in the shop, the music shop, at three shillings a week, my brother couldn't get a job at all, and so my aunties wrote and asked us to come to Leicester to live with them you see, so we did. Well Leicester at that time was the boom city of the country really. The shoes were working on full, quite busy, and the hosiery was busy, I went to get in a shop in Leicester but they were paying ten shillings (50p) a week and tuppence on sales, you know, on every pound. Well I thought I shouldn't sell much because they were going to put me on a button counter, and it didn't appeal to me, so I went in the hosiery and I went to A. W. Swann's at the time, and of course I worked there all my working time, I done all right at Swann's, it was quite a good firm.

Mrs Woodcock

Basque children

There were Basque refugee children in 1936 at Evington. Some of them were quite small. We got by on signs, hand signs, and of course ball games, I mean once anybody takes up anything like that, when you're just playing, you don't bother. I remember we had a laugh because we couldn't understand each other. I don't think they understood us, and we obviously didn't understand them. They were

alright, they played, I think it's the innocence of childhood, they just played. They were probably unhappy being in a strange country. I've no idea even how long they were here for, but I know they played alright, and the only thing I can remember about them really is swapping signatures, you know, and I had all theirs on a paper. I can remember somebody saying about the low level dive-bombings, but whether it was the children or whether it was something else, I don't know. They must have brought helpers with them, whether it was a grown up telling us, but I've got that picture in my mind of children cowering. That's all we really knew about it then.

Primrose Hall

A noble war effort

I had very close contact with the Basque refugee children who came to us. I, totally unpractical, was driven to the Technical College to learn how to cobble shoes. I came back and instructed some of my colleagues and the sixth form girls in the gentle art of cobbling. The Technical College lent us benches and knives and tools of all sorts, and we mended Basque children's shoes. It was a noble war effort! Of course, they gradually went back home, except two who were adopted here.

D. Adams

Czech refugees

Czech refugees came in 1938, mainly from Sudeten when Hitler marched in there and they had to get out quick. There were approximately twenty including wives, allowed into the county on the understanding that they would not be a charge on national or local authority funds.

They were spread around, mainly among Left Book Club members' families. Those members of the Club who did not take refugees made contributions towards the maintenance, towards those that did. The people that kept the refugees were given ten shillings a week. They had meetings of refugees every week to learn languages and for social purposes.

Albert Hall

A difficult situation

My father exported to Leicester. He started exporting at the end of the '20s or early '30s to Leicester because Mr Hubert Bergen, who was the joint founder of what was then known as the John Bull rubber company, he wanted to have glass reflectors which were put into the rubber mouldings at the back of bicycles. When the situation got difficult in Czechoslovakia my father managed to obtain a transit visa to England for eventually emigrating to Canada where he had a cousin, and that was the original plan. My parents were offered a job to manage a run down glass factory, English Glass, which Hubert Bergen had set up in Leicester. He foresaw the war coming and wanted to be independent of buying products on the continent, but it was not going too well. My parents were asked if they wanted to do this. So instead of emigrating to Canada we came to Leicester.

I do recall that people were very friendly, supportive neighbours. One has to remember that Leicester didn't actually have many immigrants. Leicester has been a very stable city even during the Depression, better perhaps than most cities. Most of us were welcomed at school. There was a little bit of bullying, but that was normal, and I was

Memorial on Peace Walk to the Leicester men who died fighting for the International Brigades during the Spanish Civil War.

reasonably able to take care of myself. There were quite a lot of refugees in Leicester, and many of them couldn't speak English of course, if they were older they had difficulties to communicate. So eventually English Glass became famous for being sent, from the Labour Exchange or wherever they came from, potential employees who couldn't speak English, could we employ them, or could the company employ them? So there were quite a lot. They were able to speak German to some of the other German supervisors. My father spoke German and another manager there could speak German as well, so German was the predominant language. A lot of them would be Jewish. I know of one who had to escape Germany because he was a Communist. The Germans were just as intent on eliminating Communists as some of the ethnic minorities.

Tom Lawson

Displaced persons

When the war finished in 1945 I was in Austria. We were encouraged to go back to Lithuania. As Lithuania was under Russian occupation, we refused to go, and we became displaced persons or political refugees. We were in the camps, ex-army camps. As we didn't want to go back to Lithuania, we had to emigrate somewhere. I met my wife, my girlfriend then, in Austria, and the groups or commissions used to come from abroad to our camp and engage some people who wanted to work abroad. The British were almost the most clever. They came first, and they took the cream of the labour. My wife was a teacher in the camps then, so she's got a job in England, and I said, well I shall follow when the chance arises for me. And so eventually they accepted me.

Meanwhile, while I was waiting to come to England, the Canadians came and they accepted me as well, because anybody who came, we just went for it, in case we won't get into somewhere else. But I decided to come to England because my girlfriend was already in England, working in Manchester. I worked in Manchester for almost a year. Meanwhile Rosalie, my girlfriend, had friends who got jobs in Leicester, so she moved from Manchester and came to work in textiles in Leicester. Then we decided to get married, and they let me leave Manchester to come to Leicester. We felt a little bit bitter when we understood that, although we weren't exactly promised, the impression was that after the war we would be free. But we were not free. We had to report to the police in Charles Street every so often, show our documents. But then we got married, and life didn't seem to be that bad.

Mr V. Kvietkauskas

Mastering the language

I came to Leicester in March 1938, and I've lived in the city ever since. My father lived here, and that's why I came, but soon the war started and my father went back, one month after the war started. I stayed here. It was my intention to go back to India in 1947, but along came the partition of India and I couldn't go because my people lost their home and everything, and they left their place and went to live in Pakistan, 200 miles away. When I first came here I couldn't speak English very well, but as soon as I mastered the language I was alright. The people, when they get to know you, are quite friendly, but it's getting to know you. From the time I came to this city I've got on very well with English people all round. I've got nothing to grumble about, nice and friendly. Of course it was up to me as well. I respect everybody, and I find that people are the

A Baisakhi Sikh Women's Day at Rushey Mead School in 1987.

same to me, very much the same, and I've enjoyed a lot of their hospitality.

Mr Abdul Haq

Something better

In Ireland I was working on land reclamation. I was a young lad of sixteen years old, and quite a few of my friends had already taken off and gone to various different parts of the world. I thought that there must be something better than draining land. As a young person with no ties, very often young people decided they might as well try England or they might as well try America. In my case there was none of my family here. I came to join some friends. I emigrated to Liverpool, which must have been one of the worst places for employment even in the 1950s. So consequently I didn't stay there very long before I moved to Birmingham. This firm offered to train me, and I eventually got a job as a hydraulic fitter. And it was in the course of that work that I was transferred from Weston-super-Mare of all places, to Leicester. And that's how I arrived here one cold damp Monday

121

Cllr Henry Dunphy during his term of office as Lord Mayor of Leicester.

morning. It wasn't the best time of the year, but having said that, when I looked around outside the station, I felt it was quite a pleasant place. There was none of the massive buildings I had seen in some other cities, and when I did ask for directions, at least I got a civilised reply, which wasn't always what I got in other places, and yes, I liked it immediately.

Henry Dunphy

Deciding where to settle

Before I came to settle here permanently in 1974, I came here for an eight week holiday in 1971 from Nairobi. I travelled all over the UK. I saw the system of this country and at that time I was impressed that, well, if I had to come to this country, I didn't have any problems deciding where to settle. So I made up my mind that if I could choose anywhere I would come and settle in Leicester. I liked Leicester much more than any other city. I'd been to London, I'd stayed in Birmingham and Preston, I'd visited Wellingborough and Coventry. I'd visited almost all the popular cities and towns. I particularly liked Leicester because, when I went to the city centre with my friends I was attracted by the flatness of the city, you see. It's very much geographically visible, with an easy approach. It's nicely built, and it's not a confusing city. Secondly, the roads leading out from the city centre are very straightforward, so I thought this would be good as well for communications in the future. And also the business system I had seen at that time was spread all over the city in different areas. I am a businessman, and I thought that if I had to come and choose a

Cllr Gordhan Parmar, Leicester's first Asian Lord Mayor.

On stage at Leicester's Caribbean Carnival in August 1994.

business I would have a much wider choice here in Leicester. Thirdly I was attracted because the Asian community was in a good number in 1970/71, so that is also one of the reasons that I came to Leicester.

Dullabhai Patel

Ninety days

The announcement came, and nobody believed it. When I came home again I heard the news, and my wife says 'we've got to go in ninety days'. I say 'no, it's not possible because he will change his mind.' We thought it was Mr Amin's joke or something like that, but after a week there started coming up some decrees, he used the word decree.

We ended up on 15 October 1972 at Stansted Airport. It was very cold. I took my first photograph because this was one of the records I wanted to keep, and I convinced the pilot to allow me to step down first from the plane so I could capture that particular photograph of us putting our first foot onto the soil of this country.

Eventually I came to Leicester. I was working for Dixon's, and there was a staff shortage in their Leicester shop. There were a lot of Indians here, and this was one of my own personal reasons why I did not want to come to Leicester, because in Uganda there was the big advertisements, 'don't come to Leicester', and this was one of the reasons why most people came over here. It's like if you tell a child not to touch a saucepan because it's hot, the child will try to touch it just to feel what it's like. So had Leicester not put up those big adverts I'm sure a lot of people would not have come to Leicester, because then in that country no one knew Leicester.

I thought it was a nice town. I found no hostility whatsoever, and it was quite a clean town. Generally the town was full of different cultures. There were Asians, Chinese, our Indian origins, and things like that. The British people, some of the people who knew of the Ugandans, they pitied us.

Maz Masru

Carnival

There was nothing in Leicester for African-Caribbean children. I wanted them to see they had a culture that was beautiful. We wanted to see their culture portrayed as good.

Elvy Morton

Reliving my childhood

When Leicester Carnival started in 1985, that first year I actually dressed up my kids in clown suits, because I wanted to relive my childhood in my children. The Carnival is ONE thing. Everybody comes to the Carnival, the rich, the poor, the down and out, the sick, all get involved. I mean, even the dead get involved, if you like, they come alive! Carnival in the Caribbean is

One of Maz Masru's photographs of refugees from Uganda arriving in Britain in 1972.

Children playing in Worthington Street in the 1990s.

everybody, who never speak to somebody in a hundred years, will speak to them on that day, because it is Carnival.

Bernard Francis

Returning to Lithuania

The very first time we went back, it was Gorbachev's time still, so Lithuania wasn't quite free, they were just thinking about breaking free. And it was a tremendous impression. I felt like the Pope, bending down and kissing the soil, but I didn't! They came to meet me, my brother was crying, men crying, I said 'men don't cry', but he did. It was very, very nice.

Mr V. Kvietkauskas

I could not recognise anything

When I went back to India, the village had changed, I didn't recognise it at all. We have a farmhouse, we have a guest house, we have a living house. When I went to the farmhouse, I didn't recognise it. The car stopped and I said 'why have we stopped here?' They said 'we're here, this is our farmhouse'. I could not recognise anything at all. It seemed small, I don't know why it seemed so small. It used to be a vast open space but this time it was so small. It looked so tiny, and very messy. The sugar canes, the maize, all that was all over the place, because there's nobody looking after the place very well. I was astounded, really, to see that it's changed, that it's so different. And certainly, because my parents and my grandparents are not there, nobody I knew. It was a very emotional feeling.

Anonymous female contributor (4)

Leicester is their home

I've always been an immigrant, always in my mind I've been an immigrant. But I think you would find that whatever immigrant group you talk to who've spent a certain number of years in this country or indeed in any other country, that when they return to wherever they came from, be it town, village or city, that they themselves will be regarded as a stranger. I tried it once and I didn't settle, and then I learnt my lesson. My family have been reared here, and they regard themselves as being from Leicester. Leicester is their home, and this is where I am till the day I die, I think.

List of Contributors

Leicester Oral History Archive (recorded 1980s):
D. M. Adams
Mr E. Andrews, born 1897
Mr W. E. Burton, born 1900
John Clarke, born 1921
Mr S. Coleman, born 1900
Joan Fenwick,
Mr W. Gough, born 1915
Albert Hall, born 1907
Primrose Hall, born 1925
Mr Abdul Haq, born 1917
Mrs Blanche Harrison, born 1917
Mr A. Holland, born 1915
Mrs Hilda Howlett, born
Mr William Lenton, born 1902
Mona Lewis, born 1902
Mr Lowe, born 1919
Albert Lynn
Bridgit Lyons, born 1929
Mrs G. Matthews, born 1908
Maz Masru, born 1947
Dr M. Millard
Mr A. Nicholls, born 1919
Beryl Richardson, born 1923
Frank Smith, born 1904
Mr G. Stacey, born 1921
Mrs C. Tebbutt
Nora Waddington
Mr Walton, born 1894
Mrs Walton
Mr A. Warren, born 1914
George White, born 1893
Mrs Woodcock
Anonymous male contributor (2)
Anonymous female contributor (3)

Community History, Leicester City Libraries (recorded 1993 onwards):
Dennis Britten
Tom Crosher

Louie Croxtall
Henry Dunphy
Bernard Francis, born 1944
Colin Green, born 1934
Cecil Harris
Freda Hales, born 1920
Harold Hammersley
Jackie Harvey
Tony Hurst
Mr R. Issitt
Tom Lawson, born 1931
Elvy Morton
Dullabhai Patel, born 1933
Dave Pick
Harry Oates
Iris Smith, born 1929
Vernon Spong, born 1925
Mr G. Wells, born 1910
Herbert Weston, born 1893
Ernie White, born 1920
Margaret Zientek
Anonymous male contributor (1)
Anonymous female contributor (1)

Clive Harrison Collection (recorded 1990s):
Patricia Russell, born 1919

Leicester City Museums Service Collection (recorded 1997 onwards):
Richard Buckley, born 1958
Marjorie Smart

East Midlands Oral History Archive (recorded 2001/02):
Jim Baker
Keith Dent, born 1936
Lesley Gill, born 1951
John Howlett, born 1932
Mark Jones, born 1961
Mr V. Kvietkauskas, born 1926
Shaftesbury Junior School Year 5 children, born 1994
Clare Speller, born 1964
Anonymous female contributor (2)
Anonymous female contributor (4)